Handling Truth

Navigating the Riptides
of
Rhetoric, Religion, Reason, and Research

SECOND EDITION

William Melvin Gardner

Logica Books

Published by
LOGICA BOOKS
PO Box 111
Fairhope, AL

Handling Truth:
Navigating the Riptides of
Rhetoric, Religion, Reason, and Research

SECOND EDITION

handlingtruth.com

ISBN 978-0-9761875-1-6

CONTENTS

DEDICATION

To Lou Cotton, Kenneth B. Melvin,
Gail P. Gardner, Jonathan Leff,
and to the memory of
George Raley and Richard F. Martin

HANDLING TRUTH

1

The Four Domains of Truth

WHAT IS TRUTH? Some people see the answer as self-evident, but for others *truth* is just a noun open to arbitrary definition. Neither of these extreme views improves our understanding. We would not disagree so often if truth were self-evident, and truth is not a vague term in need of a definition. In fact, four clear definitions are found in the traditional tests by which assertions come to be established truths.

The tests of truth emerged and are defended within the boundaries of four distinct domains of intellectual inquiry.

These four domains differ not only in their tests of truth, but also in the type of assertions they test, the qualifications of individuals who perform the tests, and the archives where confirmed truths are preserved. Because each domain performs a completely different test, a truth can be defended only in the domain or domains in which it was tested and established.

Keeping in mind that all truths have not passed the same type of test, consider the following assertions:

> All men are created equal.
> God created man.
> I think, therefore I am.
> Human beings evolved from an earlier species.

Each of these statements arose and was validated in a different domain, and each was assigned to the archives of its domain of origin. But not one of these assertions has passed the test of truth in all four domains, and therefore none is universally accepted as true.

The Four Domains

Comparison and discussion will be easier if we identify the four domains with names that reflect their respective methods for establishing truth. In the oldest domain, *Rhetorica*, statements are advanced or discredited by the process of persuasion and debate, or rhetoric. In Rhetorica, what is true always remains a matter of opinion. In the second domain, *Mystica*, truths are articles of faith or belief, arising from and tested by spiritual revelation, prophecy, sacred texts, personal enlightenment, or other mystical processes. In the third domain, *Logica*, truths are inferences or proofs that have been validated with the formal methods of logic. The fourth domain is *Empirica*, and its truths are confirmed empirical findings documented in detail in research journals.

We can now identify the domains of each of the assertions we considered earlier:

> All men are created equal—RHETORICA.
> God created man—MYSTICA.
> I think, therefore I am—LOGICA.
> Human beings evolved from an earlier species—
> EMPIRICA.

Each truth arises and is validated in only one of the four domains and may be untestable in the other three. If a truth can be tested in a second domain, it is possible or even likely that it will fail that test. A truth may receive little respect outside its home domain and may even be greeted with derision. For example, faith-healing ceremonies may amuse the elders of Rhetorica, Logica, and Empirica, but in the sacred halls of Mystica it is a generally accepted truth that prayer can cure the ill, even after physicians have given up.

In our search for truth we wander freely from one domain to another, gathering truths and incorporating them into our personal system of truths. But as we cross the border from one domain into another, we may discover conflicting truths and become confused. For example, the four domains do not agree on what constitutes a person. Is a person an individual in society, an immortal soul in a mortal body, an interacting mind and body, or an intelligent organism? What point marks the beginning of a human life, and when has that life ended? Our answers to such questions reveal which domain we trust; and if we trust more than one, we must learn to live with the contradictions.

Armed with the ability to identify the borders of the four domains, and with knowledge of the different tests of truth, anyone can transcend the confusion and see why widely accepted truths (and the people who accept them) often do not, and cannot, agree. Only if someone seeking the truth stays cloistered within one domain can the illusion of universally accepted truth be sustained. And even within the confines of a single domain, conflicting truths still arise.

Rhetorica: The Motherland

In Rhetorica, people argue endlessly about what is true and what is not. Applying the methods of persuasion and debate, proponents and opponents seek to convince their audiences and each other to accept their opinion of what is true. Arguments that prevail in public debate may become widely accepted as true. For example, after decades of public debate in democratic nations, men came to see women as mentally fit to vote—an idea they once considered preposterous. And today, few well-educated people can understand why women were ever denied such a basic right.

Some people may object to applying the term *truth* to opinions of the day, but we must accept that the term is commonly used in exactly that way. In fact, the most common first step in persuasion is to assert that you speak the truth. The U.S. Declaration of Independence, for example, contains the assertion, "We hold these truths to be self-evident...." It is likely that this confident rhetoric increased the acceptance of the political arguments that ensued.

Protocols for advancing and debating the truths of Rhetorica have been formalized in three major societal institutions: legislatures, courts, and editorial boards. In legislative bodies, parliamentary rules structure the debate that surrounds consideration of proposed laws. In the courts, forensic rules limit debate to specific charges and pertinent evidence. And among journalists, editorial rules provide guidelines for interviews, discussions, debates, and reports. The three forums differ in formal details but the goals of the persuaders are the same: they attempt to convince an audience that their assertions are true and that their opponents' assertions are false.

People who lack rhetorical skills do not fare well in formal debate, yet few of us can resist the temptation to defend the truth of our opinions when the stakes are high— and in Rhetorica the stakes are often high. The actions of legislatures create laws that regulate the lives of citizens and residents, the decisions of courts can determine who goes free and who does not, and editorial boards exert control over what the public is told about important events, occurring locally and around the world.

The importance of rhetorical skills in the pursuit and advocacy of truth becomes obvious when citizens are called to jury duty. Jurors in a criminal trial are ordered to discover what is true by witnessing a forensic debate, and then they are excused to debate with each other until a verdict can be reached. To reach a verdict of guilty in a criminal case in America, the jurors must be convinced "beyond a reasonable doubt." At this solemn and poignant moment, justice often fails. Celebrity trials have shown that jurors who lack an understanding of rhetorical methods may be easily manipulated and misled in their search for truth and justice.

Consider the so-called "trial of the century," held in Los Angeles, California in 1995, in which former football superstar and television sports commentator O. J. Simpson was found not guilty of the murder of his former wife and her friend. After months of evidence presentation and debate, the jurors sought and found truth as defined by the formal rules of justice, but like all truths in the domain of Rhetorica, their verdict passed only a test of persuasion and debate. In this media spectacle, rhyme replaced reason, and scientific facts, for example DNA evidence, were relegated to the status of "expert opinion." The judge allowed attorneys such unfettered flights of rhetoric that a guilty defendant might well have been convinced of his own innocence.

Even when the rules of debate are rigidly enforced, persuaders are still free to take liberties with truths imported from other domains. They may selectively present popular revelations or prophecies, make a mockery of the rules of reason, and misrepresent facts of history and science—all in order to promote their own arguments and win the debate. In the domain of Rhetorica, only the wisdom of the audience and strict enforcement of formal rules and procedures of debate can limit deception and debunk propaganda.

In the end, voters, jurors, and media audiences decide to accept one argument over another, and with that decision, they may assert that they have discovered the truth. And, according to the rules of Rhetorica, they have.

Mystica: The Holy Land

Children learn at an early age that there are limits to what they are allowed to doubt, to question, or to debate. In formal ceremonies, they are introduced to sacred truths that are final and certain, and are told to accept these truths on faith. They learn the truths revealed to prophets, memorize sacred verses and songs, listen to stories of religious and political struggles, and they learn that truths based on faith alone have no limits: miracles are possible, spirits can roam the earth and inhabit places and living things, and human life can be eternal.

To a skeptic, or to someone of a different faith, religious revelations may seem strange or incredible. Look at these revealed truths found in the archives of respected religions:

> The Buddha pure and like space, without shape or form, pervades all.

> Brahman, the Absolute, inhabits and totally permeates the universe, which is brought forth from its own substance.

> Allah, a supreme, personal, and inscrutable God, will punish those who turn to other gods and fail to recognize His chosen messenger, Mohammed.

> He that believeth on the Son hath everlasting life: and he that believeth not the Son shall not see life; but the wrath of God abideth on him.

Most believers would see only one of these statements—the one drawn from their own religion—as true, while the other three statements might appear to them as misguided or even blasphemous.

Truths of faith do not belong exclusively to established religion. Cult gurus and political ideologues may also offer revelations and ask prospective converts to become unquestioning, loyal followers. Any doubt expressed about the cult's or ideologue's teachings may be viewed as a personal failing, and criticism of official doctrines may be considered heresy, leading to expulsion or other extreme remedies.

Modern democracies grant their citizens the freedom to espouse and promote personal beliefs, even when those beliefs are held by a small minority or even a single individual. Whether beliefs are based in formal theology, political ideology, folklore, or personal delusions, citizens are free to assert them as absolute and final, but such assertions may be taken seriously only in the land of Mystica, where truth is always only a matter of faith.

Logica: The Land of Reason

In Logica, all assertions of truth must pass the test of reason. The Pythagorean theorem states that the square on the hypotenuse of a right triangle is equal to the sum of the squares on the other two sides. Like all geometric theorems, it is accepted as true because logical proofs were devised to test and confirm it. The truths of mathematics, geometry and philosophy are, like all reasoned truths, impervious to tests of rhetoric, faith, and research. Challenging reasoned truths in a court of law, at a religious inquisition, or in a scientific experiment would be pointless.

Over two thousand years ago, Aristotle formalized the methods of logic. Centuries later, during the Renaissance and the Age of Reason, logical methods came to provide the fundamental unifying principle for all scholarly disciplines: *Truth is revealed through reason.* Modern academics still profess Logica's truths and still apply the test of reason to each assertion of truth. If the premises are true and the argument is valid, scholars accept the resulting conclusion as true.

The truths of Logica have the distinction of being the only truths for which logical proofs are required, leading many scholars to think of them as higher truths, or even as the only truths. René Descartes, for example, did not rely on obvious evidence to confirm his own existence, but proved his existence through reason. Being unable to doubt his own doubting, he concluded that a doubter must exist—or as it is commonly expressed: "I think, therefore I am." But contrary to what Descartes seems to have assumed, logic is not the only nor the final test of truth; it is just one of four traditional methods for validating assertions. People are still free to ignore or reject formal reasoning, and thus the truths of Logica.

Empirica: The Land of Reality

In Empirica, events of nature and history are described and rigorously researched, and the findings are carefully documented. Natural events may be as simple and predictable as our shadows, as obvious as the sun, as invisible as dark matter, or as unapproachable as distant galaxies. They may be as hidden as the core of the earth, as complex as a human brain, or as abstract as time. But whatever inherent difficulties are involved, natural and historical objects, events, and processes eventually yield to the empirical methods of research, and facts are discovered and documented. In this fourth domain, truth is not subject to correction by public debates, spiritual revelations, or even logical analyses.

Researchers are notorious for flouting public opinion, popular beliefs, and sound reasoning, on their way to serendipitous discoveries about the natural world. Let us look at three individuals—Galileo Galilei, Charles Darwin, and John B. Watson—who proposed descriptive accounts of nature that dismayed politicians, clerics, and scholars of their times. Early in the seventeenth century, Galileo was led by his research findings to conclude, as had the sixteenth-century astronomer Nicolaus Copernicus, that the Creator's earth is not stationary at the center of the universe. In the final paragraphs of his 1859 book, *On the Origin of Species*, Darwin began an enduring controversy about human evolution with this simple statement: "Light will be thrown on the origin of man and his history." And in *Behaviorism* (1924/1925), Johns Hopkins Professor John B. Watson rejected the popular belief in free will by describing how human behavior is controlled by one's history of experience and current circumstances. Each of these researchers created a firestorm of public controversy, but in time the accepted view of the world and those who inhabit it was altered, facilitating progress in factual understanding of nature, including human nature, and providing a framework for a new era of research.

Scientific facts are always conditional and correctable. They are never final, complete, or beyond the possibility of error or misunderstanding. A researcher's report of some new finding is typically accompanied by caveats: the assumptions made, any limitations of the research design, and a statistical analysis of the likelihood that the findings occurred purely by chance.

Factual findings remain open to revision by future research, but they are not open to correction by public debate, mystical revelations, or armchair reasoning. Theories of science and history may indeed arise from reasoning, but only research data and findings can validate those theories, allowing them to be accepted as true in Empirica.

New research findings and discoveries often conflict with established facts, eventually leading to the amendment or rejection of those facts. For centuries it was an observed fact that the earth was stationary at the center of the universe, but the weight of controlled and recorded observations gradually overcame that erstwhile fact, and we are now quite sure that the earth is flying through space, traveling about sixty-seven thousand miles with each passing hour, and all the while spinning at more than a thousand miles per hour measured at its equator.

Facts are not personal. What we know from personal experience is not fact but our understanding of our experiences. We may assert that such observations are factual, but they have passed no test of truth, and we should not expect others to accept them as facts. Personal knowledge arises from personal experience, whereas facts must pass the test of rigorous research, documentation, and replication by qualified researchers.

Facts can never be proven. They may be widely accepted and trusted, but they always remain open to question and revision. The strongest statement any researcher can make on behalf of a specific fact or theory is that it has been repeatedly supported by published research findings in refereed scientific journals. Have researchers proven Albert Einstein's famous assertion that $e=mc^2$? No, nor can they ever "prove" it, but based on the research that has been done, and some truly earth-shaking tests, most scientists are satisfied that the expressed relationship is true.

In spite of the many limitations inherent in the domain of Empirica, newly established facts periodically redefine reality. And although scientists seldom use the word, they are indeed in search of *truth*, specifically the truth about reality—past, present, and future.

Irreconcilable Truth

The tests of truth differ greatly across the four domains, and, as a consequence, the truths of one domain often contradict the truths of another. Such contradictions can never be honestly reconciled, only accepted.

To avoid confusion, we should reserve the terms *opinion, belief, proof,* and *fact* to their respective domains, Rhetorica, Mystica, Logica, and Empirica. It would be misleading to say that researchers *believe* in evolution, because the description of evolution is not based on faith. Similarly, to say that creation is a *fact* implies that the story of creation arose as a scientific research finding. The *fact* of evolutionary change was discovered through biological and archeological research, in accordance with the methods of Empirica, whereas the story of creation was revealed in sacred scriptures of Mystica. Creationism arose as a *belief* and—unlike scientific theory—was not shaped by research findings, nor need it be altered to conform to such findings.

The masters of each domain study long and hard to earn the respect of their peers, but when they wander into the inner circles of a foreign domain, they receive only the polite regard reserved for a distinguished tourist who cannot speak the local language. The holy man leading a vigil at an archeological dig, the anthropologist observing people possessed by the Spirit at a Christian revival, the biologist on the witness stand at a murder trial, or the politician speaking to the faculty at a distinguished university are all out of their elements. They have ventured out of the domain in which they arbitrate truth, into a foreign land governed by rules they may neither understand nor respect.

Enduring disagreements about what is true and what is not are often clashes between two domains of truth. When proponents of creationism are pitted against proponents of evolution, the disagreement is not just a difference of opinion. It is a clash between the rules of Mystica and the rules of Empirica. Spiritual revelation and scientific research take us along totally different paths to truth, and we arrive not just at different truths, but different types of truth.

Clashes along the borders between domains are inevitable, and the resulting controversies endure because they cannot be resolved. Truth through mystical revelation produces *beliefs* about the natural and supernatural world, whereas the search for truth through scientific research produces *facts* of nature. Thus, the term *Christian Science,* if taken literally, would represent a contradiction. But Mystica and Empirica may peacefully coexist—even inside one head; indeed, many scientists manage to maintain a strong religious faith.

To the extent we wish to search for truth in more than one domain, we must learn to accept contradictory truths. If we expect truths to be universally accepted, we will remain blind to the primary and enduring source of many contradictions and disagreements. Only when we understand and respect the borders and rules of all four domains of truth can we hope to understand why we disagree. Or, for that matter, why we agree.

2

Rhetorica: The Motherland

TRUTH ORIGINATED IN Rhetorica, and there each individual's personal search for truth must begin. In this commonsense domain, we took our first tentative steps along the path to truth, asking questions and asserting opinions. Many of us eagerly accepted what we were told, while others began to doubt and challenge; but we all learned to share and defend the truth as we knew it—and what we knew had been learned through personal experience and instruction.

As we grew, we continued to learn by watching and doing, but we also depended on others to supply the answers. We asked and were told what, when, where, how, and why. We listened to the discussions and debates that swirled around us, and rapidly amassed an enormous repertoire of popular wisdom and commonsense.

Commonsense

There is no shortage of common sense to guide us in our daily decisions. Common sense expands to cover almost every issue, filling any gaps in our knowledge and understanding. As children, we heard thousands of adages and bits of conventional wisdom:

> There is a fine line between genius and insanity.
> Absence makes the heart grow fonder.
> Every vote counts.
> You get what you pay for.
> Nothing ventured, nothing gained.
> Storms are acts of God.
> If you try hard enough, you can succeed.
> You can believe it if you see it with your own eyes.
> If you want it done right, do it yourself.

Commonsense adages such as these guide our daily lives, and even a simple individual, armed with commonsense sayings, can explain and offer guidance on nearly every topic, from politics to personal relationships, work, money, religion, and the meaning of life. A good example of this is seen in Peter Sellers's 1979 movie *Being There*, in which a simple-minded gardener armed with the commonsense notion that world events cycle like the seasons became an advisor to the President of the United States. We laughed at the foolish president, but we also felt a little uncomfortable, for it was all too easy to imagine that such a thing could really happen, and perhaps it has.

People equipped with common sense gained through personal experiences may decide that they need no further education, since in Rhetorica the great questions of life are easily answered with clichés and generalizations. But rhetorical methods can also take us beyond common sense, to public speaking and formal debate about what is true.

Rhetorical Arts

Over two thousand years ago Aristotle defined *rhetoric* as the ability to observe in any given case the available means of persuasion. He might have added: and the use of this ability to sway the judgment of others. Rhetoric was once a popular academic discipline, and is today a talent much admired and cultivated by politicians, lawyers, and journalists.

Rhetorica remains, for most of us, an alluring domain. We respect and covet rhetorical skills and admire those public speakers who voice and defend our views in a skillful manner. Only a few people master the formal rules of debate or excel as public speakers, but many more aspire to improve their rhetorical skills. Books on public speaking and persuasion, such as Mortimer Adler's *How to Speak, How to Listen* or Reid Buckley's *Strictly Speaking*, find ready markets. Dale Carnegie's legendary *How to Win Friends and Influence*

People was one of the most widely read books in twentieth-century America, and it has remained in print for over seventy-five years. In spite of this abiding public interest in rhetorical skills, educational institutions today provide little training in the art of persuasive speech and formal debate.

A lack of understanding of rhetorical methods leaves even well-educated people vulnerable to political demagoguery and biased journalism. As we discuss and debate the rhetorical arguments of partisans, the assertions we ultimately accept as true depend on our ability to question what we hear and read. With the rapid flow of information effectively shrinking the world, cross-cultural exchanges have multiplied, and disagreements about what is true must be dealt with every day.

The word *rhetoric* has acquired a somewhat negative meaning in modern usage, but rhetoric remains the most basic method of establishing truth, practiced by all of us in some degree. It would be useful to have instruction in rhetoric reinstated in the basic college curriculum, so that students would learn to apply and critique skills such as eloquence, guile, dramatic expression, audience assessment, trust, strategy, and persuasive argument.

Eloquence

Eloquence is more than facile and forceful speech. It is speech with unity, clarity, and coherence that presents a unified theme in an orderly sequence. To be persuaded, an audience must understand what the speaker is saying, see the point, and sense a progression of ideas. The eloquent speaker will avoid jargon, digression, cliché, and repetition, since such crutches may repel rational listeners and draw attention away from the central message.

Guile

While the word *guile* may suggest dishonesty, it also has a positive meaning—it refers to reducing an audience's resistance to a message. I once witnessed a lively but complicated presentation of a new educational technique, during which the speaker showed a progressive sequence of complex graphs and charts leading up to what seemed to be his final point. He suddenly stopped and stepped back from his charts, exclaiming, "Hey, this is really beginning to make sense!" Once the laughter subsided, he had everyone's attention. The audience was beguiled and eager to hear his conclusions.

Dramatic Expression

When a speaker displays a lack of conviction or confidence, the audience may become disinterested and doubtful. In televised debates for the 2004 Democratic Party primaries in the U.S., the presidential candidates generally spoke with eloquence and guile, but most were reserved and—let's be honest—dull. Perhaps because he had little to lose, the Reverend Al Sharpton, a prominent civil rights activist, spoke with the lively emotion of personal commitment, eliciting a positive response from the audience. On the basis of dramatic appeal, he handily won every debate. His candidacy ultimately failed, but not because of a lack of rhetorical skill.

Audience Assessment

There are many rules for assessing an audience: Talk with those who arrive first, learn something about their interests, note their body language, and look for shared experiences with them. But most importantly, a speaker should take care not to speak up or down to an audience.

There is an anecdote about a high school counselor who expressed nervousness when asked by her doctor to speak at a meeting of interns about drug use among high school students. Her physician told her, "Don't worry, just speak to them as though they were a reasonably bright bunch of high school students." Then he added, "When I address high school students, I speak to them as though they are poorly trained interns." The point is a valid one. Adjust the message to your audience, but take care not to patronize or give undue credit for wisdom. Two ways to get your message rejected by an audience are to presume that its members already understand or that they cannot understand what you have to say.

Trust

First impressions matter. Personal appearance affects the trust we are willing to place in what people say. We assess the motives and competence of people largely on the basis of personal appearance and first comments, but things we have been told in advance about the speaker can also influence first impressions. If you learn that someone you're about to hear is a Nobel laureate, you may overlook any negative first impressions.

Although we tend to assess the motives and competence of a speaker within a few seconds, we often change our assessment as new facts emerge. I once had a student who dressed and spoke like a laborer, but I soon realized that he was by far the most scholarly and well-educated student in the class. I quickly set aside my first impressions and attended carefully to what he had to say, ignoring his dialect and attire.

Strategy

To be rhetorically effective, you need a plan and an objective. Do you want to alter the opinions of the audience or to encourage its members to take action—or both? How can you best attain your objective? The first step is always to gain the attention of the audience, then to show the importance of your message, and finally to indicate how each listener's actions can make a vital difference.

Let us follow the development of a strategy for a hypothetical presentation. Suppose the goal is to increase support for The United Nations Population Fund, an organization dedicated to population control on a worldwide level. A little-known but startling fact can be presented to get the attention of the audience: World population grew very little until 1800, when it was approaching the one billion mark. Over the next century it began to grow rapidly and reached 1.6 billion by 1900. While a 60% increase in just a hundred year was shocking, it was only a prelude. During the twentieth century, world population nearly quadrupled, from 1.6 billion in 1900 to 6.1

billion in 2000, with another billion people being added every twelve years thereafter.

Once the audience's attention has been gained with such startling figures, the problem can be stated objectively. The speaker can point out that water for irrigation and land for farming are significantly depleted each year. In some years, more grain is consumed than is produced, reducing worldwide reserves to a few weeks' supply. If world population continues to increase at the current rate, while farmable land and water for irrigation continue to be depleted, sharp rises in the price of grain are inevitable. History has shown that when grain crops fail, the price of bread quickly doubles, and then doubles again. In poor, unstable countries, the price and scarcity of grain has already led to widespread malnutrition, suffering, and starvation.

The speaker might then advise the audience about the general lack of governmental concern for the growth in world population, and provide names and contact information for government officials, so that members of the audience can urge their elected representatives to support The United Nations Population Fund.

Rhetorical Argument

The basic rhetorical argument is the *enthymeme* (pronounced *en-thi-meem*). We often resist new or novel words, but this term is a valuable addition to everyone's vocabulary, useful in separating rhetorical discussions from dialectical discussions. Unlike dialectical arguments that use logic to solve problems and discover the truth, enthymemes use logic to persuade. Enthymemes are typically logically incomplete arguments that allow listeners to fill in the missing premise, and the premises of an enthymeme need not be true, only plausible.

Consider the following enthymeme: *Mr. Jefferson cannot be elected president; he is an atheist.* Listeners who heard this incomplete argument when it was advanced in 1800 were left to fill in the missing premise: *An atheist cannot be elected president.* This completed argument was valid:

> An atheist cannot be elected president.
> Mr. Jefferson is an atheist.
> Therefore, Mr. Jefferson cannot be elected president.

Many people agreed that an atheist could not be elected president, and many believed Mr. Jefferson was an atheist, but these propositions were, at best, only possibly true. Since Mr. Jefferson was in fact elected as the third president of the United States, we know in retrospect that at least one of the two premises leading to the conclusion was false: Either Mr. Jefferson was not an atheist, or an atheist could be elected president.

Although enthymemes take the form of logical arguments, their premises and the conclusion remain open to dispute. For example, one could argue that Mr. Jefferson was a deist rather than an atheist, or one could argue that voters see a president's religious views as unrelated to his moral and intellectual capacity to lead their nation.

There are many ways to categorize enthymemes. Perhaps the most useful is to divide them into two general categories: supportive arguments and refutations. In formal debate, one side provides arguments in favor of a resolution while the other side provides arguments to refute the resolution.

In a criminal trial, the role of the defense attorney is to dispute the prosecutor's arguments made in support of conviction. Generally, defendants do not have to prove their innocence, but need only discredit the evidence or the arguments presented by the prosecution. Let us return to the trial of O. J. Simpson, in which defense attorney Johnny Cochran uttered his now famous rhyming couplet about the bloody glove: "If it doesn't fit, you must acquit." Cochran was rightly confident that jurors would complete his enthymeme:

> The bloody glove fits the murderer.
> The bloody glove does not fit the defendant.
> Therefore, the defendant is not the murderer.

Attorney Cochran's contention that the glove did not fit the defendant was not a demonstration of Mr. Simpson's innocence, but an attack on the prosecution's evidence of guilt. Cochran's clever enthymeme was devised to cast doubt on, and bring about reconsideration of, the prosecutor's evidence of guilt, even though the second premise of his enthymeme was far from certain. It might, in fact, be quite difficult, even impossible, for a prosecuting attorney to put a tight glove on a defendant whose freedom depends on its not fitting.

Faulty Arguments: Weak Rhetoric

Irrational arguments are often useful in swaying an uncritical audience. Most of us have at least some understanding of three types of faulty arguments: *argumentum ad hominem, begging the question,* and *straw-man arguments.* Generally, however, only people who master the tactics of Rhetorica are able to expose these false arguments as they are put forth in debates and discussions.

Argumentum ad hominem refers to arguments that attack the speaker without addressing the truth or falsity of the speaker's assertions. Consider the following assertion: *Only immoral people make statements in favor of war.* Obviously, the objective is to discredit arguments in favor of war by attacking the morals of proponents of those arguments. But the validity of an argument does not rest on the credibility of its source, so criticizing the proponents is irrelevant and misleading. But that does not make these tactics ineffective. One need only note the broad appeal of the forty-fifth U.S. President's personal attacks on those who criticize or question his actions.

Begging the question is the term for a faulty argument in which the conclusion is nothing more than a restatement of a premise. Consider the following argument: *Because colleges have lowered their admission standards, students with lower admissions scores are now admitted to college.* If we are willing to accept the proposition that admission standards have been lowered, then we have already granted the "conclusion" that students with lower admissions scores are now eligible for admission. What appears at first glance to be a valid conclusion is no more than a repetition of the original proposition—begging the question. {Note: the term "begging the question" is often incorrectly used to mean raising a question.}

A *straw-man argument* is introduced when an opponent's position is conveniently reworded to open it to attack. If your opponent argues that we can reduce gasoline consumption by increasing gasoline tax, you can restate his position by saying: "He wants to increase the price of gasoline," when in fact what he is advocating a decrease in the consumption of gasoline. If your opponent is says he supports the ACLU, you can say he supports the Nazi movement, because the ACLU has defended the civil rights of members of a Nazi group. By misstating your opponent's position, you turn his argument into a vulnerable and easily defeated "straw man."

Rhetoric often contains breeches of logic, such as *argument ad hominem, begging the question,* and *straw-man arguments,* but such faulty reasoning does not necessarily diminish the persuasiveness of the arguments. Even the lowest form of *argumentum ad hominem*—childish name-calling—can persuade an uncritical audience.

Demagogues do not just promote their views with irrational arguments, they intentionally exploit the ignorance, prejudices, and emotions of the audience. While these techniques may fail to sway rational and skeptical people, they can be quite effective with others. Political advisors are expert in turning candidates into demagogues, and some candidates need little coaching. In this "post-truth era" demagoguery has become so prevalent that it is excused as normal politics.

World events in the first half of the twentieth century should have taught us that a charismatic demagogue can easily convert a modern democracy into a totalitarian state, but few people remember that it was demagoguery and propaganda that led to the Holocaust and World War II. In the postwar years, people cried "Never again!" But that is now forgotten, and, as George Santayana warned, "Those who cannot remember the past are condemned to repeat it."

Bias and Partisanship in Rhetorica

We know what difficulties people encounter when they attempt to escape the influences of their own experiences and personal interests. The *voir dire* process for striking jurors in court trials is intended to allow attorneys to exclude prospective jurors whose personal history or current circumstance might predispose them toward a decision unrelated to the evidence. The *voir dire* process does not suggest that jurors do not try to be objective, but admits that all of us have personal biases, regardless of our desire to remain open-minded and objective.

We rightly distrust jurors who have an apparent conflict of interest, regardless of their assurances that their needs and interests will not affect their interpretation of evidence. We know that we cannot depend on jurors to recognize and admit their own prejudices, especially prejudices that are unpopular, immoral, or illegal.

Few criminal cases since the murder of American civil rights activists in the 1960s have publicly revealed more ethnic bias than the O. J. Simpson murder trial discussed earlier. To the defendant's family, and to many others who identified with him, the not-guilty verdict was justified; but to observers who identified with the white victims and their families, the verdict appeared biased. African-Americans who had long experienced prejudicial law enforcement saw conspiracy among white police officers, whereas many whites saw racial chauvinism in the African-Americans who cheered the verdict. Under the spotlight of the media, both sides expressed indignation at any suggestion that they were biased, yet members of each group were quick to accuse the other side of precisely that.

We have all heard comments such as, "He looked guilty to me." Judges and jurors may deny that their decisions are influenced by the defendant's appearance, yet research has shown that in cases involving blue-collar crime, a well-dressed and well-groomed defendant is less likely to be found guilty or, if found guilty, is more likely to receive a light sentence. Aware of this bias, defense attorneys wisely advise their clients to remain silent, dress appropriately, and maintain modest grooming. Many potential jurors freely admit social bias against unattractive or inappropriate attire, although they might still deny that such things would influence them as jurors.

Political biases are enumerated in party platforms, and candidates present their loyalty to their party's platform as evidence of personal integrity. Candidates label themselves by biases they hold, such as "conservative Christian," or "pro-labor progressive." The message is clear, their biases flaunted. Candidates who try to keep an open mind about controversial issues are often described by their opponents as evasive, indecisive, or wishy-washy.

Political action groups spend millions of dollars to influence the outcome of elections and in the process polarize public opinion. For example, in America mutual opposition invigorates both the Pro-Life and Pro-Choice movements, and as a consequence, members of both groups express their opinions more stridently. For one side, a single human cell, a fertilized egg, is defined as a person—body and soul. For the other group, human life begins only at the point of independent biological viability. Such extremes of opinion inflame the political debate and make compromise difficult, if not impossible, with neither group willing to concede an inch. Truly neutral politicians, who see prenatal development as a gradual transition through stages from a zygote to a human being, would be seen as enemies by both camps, accused by one side of disregarding human life and by the other of abandoning the rights of women.

Candidates who attempt to keep an open mind, so that they can negotiate and reach compromise, are rare. Most politicians feel forced to take sides on hot issues, and to accept campaign contributions and endorsements earned by their expressed biases. And because their biases are admitted, voters and contributors alike can support candidates who share their prejudices. This can take the focus off the personal and professional qualities of the candidates, including experience, truthfulness, knowledge, reasonableness, and morality. People who share the biases of a partisan candidate may defend the candidate as a strong and gifted leader with a unique ability to restore the nation to greatness, while the opposition may describe the candidate as a demagogue seeking autocratic power.

Prejudice and bias are natural and predictable human characteristics. Only by rigorously enforcing traditional and formal rules of order and debate can personal prejudices and biases be moderated and common ground found.

Rules of Debate

Free democratic societies maintain three forums for the resolution of differences of opinion: courts, legislatures, and editorial boardrooms. People holding opposing views routinely meet in these arenas and attempt to resolve their disputes. On occasion they even reach agreement on what should be accepted as true.

Judicial Methods

Criminal and civil courts provide rule-governed forums for the adversarial debate of evidence and determination of whether specific laws or agreements have been violated. To insure prompt and focused debate, a body of rules limits courtroom discussion to the pertinent evidence and the defendant's actions relevant to the charges. The judge's mandate is to guide the rhetorical search for truth, and to insure that the jury abides by forensic rules of debate and reaches a deliberated verdict.

Forensic rules of debate have historically been the only satisfactory means for achieving impartial enforcement of law. Twentieth-century governments have reluctantly accepted certain technical aspects of modern science into court systems, but forensic debate continues to guide the search for truth in judicial deliberations and decisions.

In *Frye v. United States* (1923), the court ruled that the results of a polygraph test were not admissible as evidence. The ruling stated that scientific evidence is admissible in court only when the methods used are generally accepted in the appropriate scientific community. In other words, science-based evidence is allowed in American courts only when it is judged acceptable, and then only under the heading of "expert *opinion*."

Attorneys and judges steadfastly defend the merits of forensic debate as a technique for finding truth, but to the devout believer, to the unbending logician, or to the dedicated scientist, what passes for truth-seeking activity in court may be seen as little more than a circus. To the devout Christian, the ultimate truth resides with God, so jurors should pray for guidance. To the logician, a lawyer's emotional appeals and verbal incantations are irrelevant diversions from valid reasoning. To the scientist, replicated observations, rigorously recorded data, and conditional probabilities determine what is accepted as fact, so forensic rules that allow jurors to base judgments of guilt on eye-witnesses reports may appear foolish. In scientific research eyewitness testimonies are labeled "anecdotal evidence."

What the elders of other domains think about judicial proceedings is of no concern to the courts. In the stately halls of democratic justice, truth will continue to be arbitrated by judges with ordinary citizens serving as jurors, not by clerics, scholars, or scientists.

Parliamentary Procedures

Legislatures provide a broader and looser forum for persuasion and debate. Ideally, political debate insures that all discussion is exhausted and that all consequences and alternatives are considered. The objective is to negotiate compromise and, consequently, to obtain broad-based support for legislative actions.

As common as constitutional democracy is today, we may assume that the practices evolved over the ages, but that is not the case. Constitutional democracy was, arguably, introduced to the modern world in 1787 as a consequence of a colonial revolution. The Constitution of the United States introduced a secular form of government in which all laws would be established by a vote of publicly elected representatives, without authorization by a monarch, autocrat, oligarchy, or priestly authority. Over the next two centuries, many constitutional democracies formed around the world and, by the end of the twentieth century, public political debate had become the preferred method for establishing law in nearly all countries with a free press.

The trend toward free expression of political opinion seemed inexorable, yet noteworthy exceptions continue to exist. Law still emanates from a central authority in many countries where political truth may be tested and established by doctrinal faith or by the dictates of one person or an oligarchy. Today, in this age of electronically spread misinformation there has been a resurgence of nationalistic and autocratic demagogues, and many democracies struggle to endure.

In spite of setbacks, modern democratic laws still provide a stable framework that allows voters to select representatives who are sworn to uphold laws. Elected officials may debate *for* their constituents, following the mandate of public opinion, or they may debate *with* their constituents, in an attempt to lead public opinion. Successful politicians typically choose the former, safer route.

In democratically elected legislative bodies, the rules of rhetoric are formal and the outcomes are binding. Dedicated partisans attempt to persuade colleagues by arguing about which assertions are true and which are false. The outcome of such debates can have far-reaching consequences, determining whether a nation goes to war or seeks compromise, what rights individuals and corporations have, how taxes are levied, which policies and programs are launched, and which public services are made available.

Editorial Rules

In addition to forensic and legislative forums, we have a third, less-binding forum that guides the dissemination of information. Stories reported in the news media are typically based on the opinions of people interviewed and the personal observations of reporters, with the finished product subjected to editorial review and modification to insure conformity with the publication's editorial standards. Often, however, editorial modification produces news stories that are tainted with the personal biases of management.

Journalists generally take pride in following editorial rules, and may even claim that they report only the *facts*, but stories must undergo confirmation by historians before that term can be rightly applied. Many journalistic reports eventually pass the scrutiny of historical review, but many do not.

In the early 1970s, U.S. President Richard M. Nixon stonewalled the press corps as it inquired into details of a possible cover-up of the Watergate burglary. The cover-up was eventually exposed and Nixon's presidency toppled as a consequence. Since then, American reporters have been more aggressive and speculative, often seeking to elicit radical opinions in order to generate controversy, rather than to describe and explain events. In a syndicated column in March, 1999, Georgie Anne Geyer voiced exactly this complaint by lamenting political reporters' tendency to critique answers they receive or to substitute their own opinions. She said that journalists had shifted toward a "free-floating anti-authority mood," a distrust of authorities that leads to the expectation that only "conflict and confrontation" can deliver truth.

Actually, from the earliest weekly newspapers to today's almost instantaneous twenty-four-hour reporting, journalists have sought truth in conflicting opinions, and have contributed their own interpretations of events as well. Stirring up a debate has always been easier and has earned higher audience ratings than conducting research rigorous enough to earn the historical label of *fact*.

With the advent of cable news channels, we now have instant analysis of the news by discussion groups made up of reporters, experts, commentators, politicians, and celebrities. Panel-show moderators exert little editorial restraint, and discussions frequently digress into shouting matches with all participants talking at once. When that occurs, the rhetorical path to truth is lost. In these entertainment/news programs, well-known political partisans and contentious commentators are the headliners, and the rules of debate are unclear. With no mandate to reach a resolution, the moderator's objective drifts toward evoking and inflaming partisan debate, and thereby generating "breaking news."

In fairness, most mainstream journalists do their jobs well. Their audiences are exposed to opinions, analyses, and debates, and can, if they wish, reach thoughtful decisions about what is true. Editors and reporters may harbor political biases, or subscribe to popular opinion, or overdo lurid stories, but a free press remains the essential voice of democracy. Just as a dictatorship cannot survive a free press, a democracy cannot survive without one. When we hear the press referred to as the "enemy of the people," we are witnessing an autocratic demagogue's frontal assault on democratic government.

Put broadly, the methods and rules of Rhetorica have made possible the modern world of democracy, with open courts and a free flow of ideas. The truth of political assertions, legal arguments, and news reports can always be disputed, but their truth should be disputed only in accordance with established rules of sanctioned debate, and not adjudicated in unruly shouting matches among partisans.

3

Mystica: The Holy Land

ALL TRUTHS BASED on faith fall within the domain of Mystica, from the formal doctrines of major religions to the teachings of cult leaders, cultural myths, superstitions, and even delusions. Mystica's truths are accepted on faith alone and presented as absolute and final.

While the methods of Rhetorica, Logica and Empirica play no essential role in establishing Mystica's truths, they are often employed to promote and defend faith-based truths. To defend their beliefs, people who believe in God may appeal to rhetorical debate, logical arguments, or

research findings, even though their belief in God was
originally based on faith alone and needs only faith to
validate it.

Religious Faith

The beliefs of established religions are typically taught
in formal settings, such as churches, monasteries, and
seminaries, and are reinforced in cultural rites and rituals,
holiday celebrations, literature, and music. Long before
children can understand the meaning of religious doctrines,
they are taught that faith is a virtue, and that religious truths
must be accepted on faith alone. Regardless of their ages and
levels of understanding, children are counted as members of
their parent's faith, and as they mature they are usually
initiated into that faith.

When we speak of world religions today, we must
acknowledge the numerical dominance of Christianity and
Islam. These religions are relatively young, but half the
world's seven billion people are identified as belonging to
one or the other. There are more than two billion Christians
and more than one and a half billion Muslims. The relatively
rapid rise to prominence experienced by these two groups
can be attributed, at least in part, to aggressive proselytizing
and a history of conquests.

Judaism stands among the oldest and most influential
religions, but today there are fewer than 15 million members
of the Jewish faith. The major eastern religions—Hinduism,
Buddhism, Daoism, and Confucianism—are thousands of
years old, and each has hundreds of millions of followers.

But only Hinduism, with almost a billion followers, approaches the size of Islam or Christianity.

Rejecting Science

In the view of many religious believers, all truth is a matter of what one chooses to believe. For example, some Christians categorize the scientific understanding of evolution as a faith that they call "Darwinism." In their 2009 book, *In Praise of Doubt*, Peter Berger and Anton Zijderveld use terms such as "scientism" and "evolutionism" to cast science as an alternative faith, rather than an alternative to faith.

Now that oil in the Middle East has brought Islam to the attention of the entire world, westerners who look to reason and science for truth often struggle to understand radical Islamism. They find it difficult to accept that Muslims steeped in religious fundamentalism place their absolute truths of faith far above the relative truths of human reason and research.

In Yann Martel's popular novel, *Life of Pi* (2002), the main character Pi, a boy growing up in India, searches for religious enlightenment. Pi speaks for many religious believers and spiritualists when he presents spiritual revelation as a higher form of truth that explains things that reason and science cannot. Pi describes the people with whom he studied and worked as either agnostics "...in the thrall of reason, that fool's gold for the bright..." or as scientists, who are atheists "...preoccupied with sex, chess and baseball...." The informed believer is presented, by comparison, as one who stands above and apart from the glitz of reason and the commonness of science.

Fundamental Christians, such as the late Reverend Billy Graham, have overtly promoted faith as transcendent over other domains of truth. Graham stated in a syndicated column (November, 2010) that there is no conflict between science and faith if they are properly understood. Science, he said, deals with physical reality, things that we can see and touch, but it cannot inform us about spiritual reality—those things that can't be seen or touched. Graham then argues that God and the human soul, things of the spiritual world, are more "real" than the things we can see around us.

Contrary to Graham's assertion, there are indeed conflicts between science and religion. Religions promote many mystical beliefs about the tangible world that are inconsistent with the factual findings of science. The question is, when conflict is encountered, which do we accept as true—the scientific or the faith-based? Graham reveals his answer when he asserts that God is more real that the real world.

Opium of the People?

Religions typically offer some form of relief from the stresses of daily life. Christians say that believing in Jesus absolves them of sin. By following the teachings of Mohammed, Muslims believe that men can be delivered to a joyous afterlife. Buddhists believe that the path of self-improvement leads to a cessation of suffering. By accepting religious guidance and enlightenment, believers transcend the travails of life and gain the security and contentment provided by the removal of uncertainty.

To the extent that religious faith lifts the burden of doubt, relieves worry and pain, and brings contentment, religion may be, as Karl Marx asserted, "the opium of the people." But if religion is in some metaphorical sense an opiate, it is not *just* an opiate. Most great civilizations of the past were anchored in religious faith, and the creation of many enduring cultural edifices and institutions has been motivated by religious faith. The religions of Abraham served as organizing forces for civilizations of the Middle East, northern Africa, Europe, and beyond. Similarly, religions such as Hinduism, Sikhism, Buddhism, Daoism, Confucianism, and Shintoism united great cultures of the Eastern World.

Leaders of some early civilizations were presented as gods, or as rulers ordained by God. Egyptian pharaohs became god-kings, and the Pope crowned Roman Emperors. Even in the twentieth century, emperors and monarchs were often seen as gods or as ordained into the service of God. Japan's Emperor Hirohito was considered to be a living god, and the Monarch of the United Kingdom carries the additional title of Supreme Governor of the Church of England and Defender of the Faith. Their association with divine authority gave these rulers the stature to unite and lead their people through times of destruction, deprivation, and sacrifice.

The spread of democracy during the last few centuries has brought a decline in the use of faith to validate the authority of leaders, but the tendency of politicians to seek divine support still abounds. The United States introduced secular democracy (that is, constitutional separation of church and state) to the Western World, but even in the materialistic society of today, most American political candidates continue to publicly avow beliefs and values in line with the Christian faith and claim that their service to the people will be "informed" by their faith. In a debate on December 13, 1999, when the Republican candidates for President of the United States were asked to name their favorite political philosopher, George W. Bush (who would go on to win the election) answered "Christ." Similarly, during the May 3, 2007 presidential debate, in response to the question "Do you believe [sic] in evolution?" three Republican candidates indicated they did not, revealing their faith in the biblical story of creation. Even in secular democracies, avowal of religious faith can be essential for election to high positions of leadership.

Commitment to Faith

When people commit to believe in the teachings of a specific religion, their acceptance into that community of faith is typically recognized in formal ceremonies. They then embark on a lifelong process of enlightenment and transformation. Novices seldom know or understand all the teachings of their chosen religion, but dedicate themselves to the process of learning and believing what they find in the sacred texts of their faith. For example, Christians may accept the Holy Bible on faith, even before they have read it in its entirety and attempted to understand it.

Many religions are exclusionary. When people make a commitment to the beliefs of an exclusionary faith, it is as if the door locks behind them, and the exits are marked "Danger." Both Christianity and Islam, for example, require members to forsake all other religions and adhere only to the tenets of *the one true faith*. Christians who stray from faith may be confronted with the threat of eternal suffering and the loss of Christian fellowship. In some Muslim communities, those who are attracted to other faiths may face social rejection, harsh punishment, or even execution.

Experiencing Spiritual Forces

Adherents to most religious faiths believe in an alternative spiritual world, and may believe that they experience spiritual forces. As noted earlier, some Christian fundamentalists may claim that the spiritual world is more real than the physical world described by science.

When we are in the altered state of consciousness known as dreaming, what we imagine may be compelling, even if it is absurd. As we awake, drifting in and out of sleep, we may have difficulty differentiating dreams from actual events, and ask ourselves "Did that really happen, or did I dream it?" Similarly, for those who believe in the Christian spiritual world, quotations from holy texts may evoke clear images of heaven, angels, and God. Within the context of psychological events, such human imagining differs only subtly from the actual perception of material objects, but from a theological perspective imagining is often treated as a mystical experience, not as a naturally occurring psychological phenomenon.

Christians who believe in the supernatural aspects of religion may believe they feel the presence of God or hear His voice—or even see His face. And within the domain of Mystica, these experiences may be treated not as dreams, imaginings, or hallucinations, but as divine revelations. When someone asserts, "God exists, I know because I have felt His presence," the truth of the assertion is validated by the unquestioning belief in spiritual experiences.

A Domain Divided

The truths of Mystica are limited only by human imagination, so we should not expect different faiths to have compatible tenets of truth, but because people of different faiths share similar life experiences, it is not surprising that there are unifying beliefs among the major religions of the world. Such agreements, however, stand in contrast to the many contradictory beliefs between and within religions.

Within each faith, multiple interpretations of doctrine open the door to disputes and conflicts, and lasting schisms may emerge. To combat this tendency, religions suppress divergence within their ranks by requiring followers to demonstrate acceptance of the authorized interpretation of the sacred texts. By specifying what is to be believed and how believers should dress and act, religious leaders retain control over hundreds of millions of believers.

In many faiths, a believer who openly doubts the authorized doctrine or who fails to perform prescribed rituals may face warnings and sanctions. For example, Martin Luther's questioning of priestly practices in 1521 led to his excommunication from the Roman Church. In return, however, Martin Luther spawned the Protestant movement, which in effect excommunicated the Pope.

Cults

When believers organize around the teachings of a self-appointed leader or a new doctrine of faith, a cult is born. Like religions, cults are made up of like-minded believers, but they differ from religions in size, longevity, formality, stability, and organizational complexity. A cult is typically personality-centered and may disband when its leader dies or is discredited.

Not all cults form around spiritual or ideological beliefs. A political populist or a celebrity may attract a cult of followers. Dictatorial leaders who control communications media can ban dissent and create a political cult of personality. Such cults are typically sustained by the relentless dissemination of propaganda.

To say that cult members share a common delusion may be an overstatement, but it is no exaggeration to say that a cult is a community with a shared reality that an uninvolved observer would likely see as delusional. The Polish aphorist, Stanislaw J. Lec, said, "All our separate fictions add up to joint reality." Cult members exemplify this statement by believing that their shared views constitute reality.

Because religious cults lack broad public support, they are vulnerable. Their leaders tend to isolate followers from outside influences and may require them to take some form of loyalty oath. Cult leaders are ever watchful for traitors, infiltrators, and nonbelievers. When cult members show signs of weakening commitment, they may be dealt with promptly, either brought back in line or cast out of the group.

When new converts join a cult, its beliefs are socially validated, and as a result cults naturally tend to proselytize. As their membership increases cults gain social prominence and respectability. Scientology began in 1952 under the guidance of L. Ron Hubbard and became a successful cult that claims to be a religion. Its promotion of beliefs at odds with science and reason and the beliefs of dominant religions has brought public criticism. Like any other cult, its survival will depend upon keeping its teachings and leaders isolated from public scrutiny and criticism.

Many people find it surprising that all religions began as cults. From humble origins, ancient cults grew in size and formality, and in time attained the status of accepted religions. Christianity, for example, took decades to advance beyond its origins as a small Hebrew cult. Without the leadership and teachings of Paul of Tarsus, it is unlikely that Christianity would have survived and spread across the Roman Empire.

Many religions trace their roots to a cult leader who was immortalized as a prophet or messiah. The teachings of Confucius, Siddhartha, Jesus, and Mohammed first attracted small bands of like-minded believers, but with our historical perspective we now see each of these prophets as the originator of a great religion. Had their messages not resonated well through time, their faiths might have faded into the shadows of history—as most of their contemporaneous cults did.

Since leaders of established religions are quick to identify them as false prophets, cult leaders must walk a tightrope, rejecting established religions but taking care not to overstep into blasphemy that could provoke reprisals. Many cult leaders have felt the hot breath of inquisitors and persecutors, and some, including Jesus and the Shiite prophet al-Husayn, were martyred for their teachings. Paradoxically, martyrdom gave their messages historical status that probably would not have been attained if their lives had been spared.

Defense of Faith

While they cannot test the truths of Mystica, rhetorical arguments are often employed in the defense of beliefs. Each religion may develop an impenetrable rhetorical defense, such as, "The Lord works in a mysterious way His wonders to perform." Such rhetorical tactics can provide a final answer to troubling questions.

Another modern rhetorical tactic is to shift the discussion from a defense of a faith to an attack on reason and science. With these and similar rhetorical devices, believers defend their faith without actually engaging in the give-and-take of authentic debate.

The religions of Abraham have demonstrated repeatedly that a religion survives best when it has the protection of an army. For all the claims that the teachings of Judaism, Christianity, and Islam advocate peace among neighbors, that peace is usually buttressed by physical force. Under the banner of their God, Jews, Christians, and Muslims often engage in religious wars.

In times of peace, religious moderates may disassociate from the militant fundamentalists of their faith. But as Sam Harris suggests in *The End of Faith* (2004), when physical defense is required, it is extreme fundamentalists who fight most ardently to insure the survival of their religion and, incidentally, to insure the survival of moderates who espouse the peaceful principles of their faith.

National armies may act to insure the survival of major religions, while a cult may rely on the more limited protection of a guarded compound. David Koresh's Branch Davidians provide a tragic example of the armed defense of a cult. In February of 1993, when agents from the U.S. Bureau of Alcohol, Tobacco, and Firearms tried to enter the Branch Davidian compound near Waco, Texas, they encountered guards with automatic weapons. In the ensuing battle, four agents and six members of the cult were killed. A fifty-day siege followed and ended in a fire that destroyed the compound and killed Koresh and seventy-six of his followers, including at least twenty children.

Holy wars between conflicting faiths date back to biblical times and before. The crusades of the eleventh, twelfth, and thirteenth centuries marked the peak of the conflict between Christians and Muslims—a conflict that continues sporadically today. In more recent times, Muslim-Christian conflicts fueled the war between Serbia and Kosovo and civil war in Sudan.

In the twentieth century the greatest threat to some religions came not from other religions, but from faith-based political ideologies that denounced religions. The communist ideology embraced by Russia led to a suppression of all religions across the Soviet empire, while in Germany Nazi ideology selectively vilified members of the Jewish faith, culminating in the systematic extermination of six million Jews. Japanese soldiers' sense of superiority over the conquered Koreans and Chinese can be in part attributed to their Shinto faith.

Exorcising Beliefs

The domain of Mystica exerts far more control over individual behavior than does any other domain. Parents, fearful that differing beliefs might permanently divide families, steel their children against the teachings of other faiths and cults by warning them of false prophets. When those efforts fail and the children do join an unacceptable cult, parents have gone so far as to kidnap their estranged children, in an effort to "rescue" them.

The term *brainwashing* has been applied to the methods cults use to inculcate new members, whereas the process used to overcome or reverse such unacceptable convictions is known as *deprogramming*. The methods of brainwashing and deprogramming are remarkably similar: isolate and indoctrinate. Brainwashing and deprogramming rely on kindness and social acceptance to set the tone, but warnings and even coercion may be used to extract a commitment. The commitment phase is typically charged with emotion and may involve physical restraint.

Formal deprogramming of cult members is sometimes successful, but it can also be unnecessary. Converts may of their own accord break away from cults. In times of personal conflict and stress, or when leaders lose their moral or intellectual authority, followers may simply undergo a loss of faith.

By teaching spiritual awareness, love, celebration, creativity, meditation, and laughter, the Indian guru Bhagwan Shree Rajneesh attracted many followers to his commune in Oregon in the 1980s. His followers began to drift away, due in part to reports of the Bhagwan's all-too-mortal excesses in sex, drugs, and automobiles. When the Bhagwan was charged with a series of serious crimes and deported, the cult was transformed into the Osho International Meditation Resort.

Whether believers are members of a cult or an established religion, their faith may wane. Loss of faith may be enduring or short-lived, but it always starts with a question and ends with growing doubt. Many once-devout members break totally with their faith and turn to other religions or cults—or become religious skeptics and turn to the truths of other domains.

Over the past few centuries, Mystica has lost an increasing fraction of believers to the lures of reason and science. Rhetorica also attracts many people who drift away from religious faith. Over time, however, some doubters regain faith and return to their religion.

The Mythical and the Mysterious

In addition to religious and ideological doctrines of faith, but still within Mystica's realm of truth, are the less significant beliefs in myths, mysterious forces, and magic. In most cultures parents enrich the lives of their children with tales of magical beings. American children are told about fairy godmothers, Santa Claus, the Easter Bunny, and the Tooth Fairy. Children eventually, and sometimes with melancholy, begin to question and doubt childhood beliefs. Later, they may mourn the loss of these innocent and magical times of their lives.

Western cultures teem with fictional peoples: tiny people such as leprechauns, fairies, elves, trolls, gnomes, sprites, and hobbits; transformed humans such as witches, werewolves, vampires, and ghosts; evil spirits, demons and gremlins; and pseudoscientific spooks, including Frankenstein's monster, radiation-mutated creatures, space aliens, and robotic humanoids. Imaginary beings populate Western cultural lore, and a few people believe them to be real, or at least possible. As the old story goes, an elderly Irish lady, asked if she believed in leprechauns, replied, "Sure and of course I don't, but they're all out there just the same."

Belief in witchcraft, voodoo, spiritualism, divination, palmistry, astrology, clairvoyance, telepathy, precognition, psychokinesis, channeling, numerology, charms, and other magical forces is still found almost everywhere, sometimes in surprising places—such as the White House. First Lady Nancy Reagan was known to consult an astrologer to determine propitious timing for her husband's official activities. Even intellectually sophisticated people, normally skeptical of mysterious forces, may quietly harbor small superstitions, such as feeling lucky or jinxed. They may be very picky about their lottery ticket numbers, even when they know, on a rational level, that their so-called "lucky numbers" have no enhanced probability of winning.

Sometimes folklore and cultural traditions run afoul of religious teachings, in which case there can be strong reactions. For example, at Halloween most Americans see the celebration of witches, ghosts, and pumpkins as a harmless tradition, but some Christian fundamentalists condemn the holiday as a celebration of the devil and refuse to allow their children to participate.

Many people still believe in cultural myths of mysterious forces. Folk cures have diminished in popularity over the last two centuries, but have by no means disappeared. "Snake Oil" may be hard to find, but there are markets for all sorts of dietary supplements, herbs, tonics, charms, magnets, and bracelets. Faith-healing, reflexology, mineral baths, aroma therapies, purifications, balancing, rituals, harmonic healing and a variety of other similar interventions and treatments are represented as cures for medical problems and pains, or as a means to improve health and increase strength, happiness, or longevity.

Believers in alternative medical treatments often cite research that "proves" the efficacy of their cures. But believers are often naïve about the rigors and caveats of scientific research. The tests to which they refer may be little more than selected cases, anecdotal reports, or supportive testimonials from experts or celebrity believers. When an alternative medical treatment fails the test of rigorous scientific research, it is typically the research finding that is rejected by believers and practitioners, not faith in the treatment.

The National Center for Complementary and Alternative Medicine was established in the United States in 1998 as a center within the National Institutes of Health, and in 2014 it was renamed the National Center for Complementary and Integrative Health. Its original mandate was to fund research into the effects of "diverse medical and health care systems, practices, and products that are not generally considered part of conventional medicine." This controversial agency spent hundreds of millions of dollars on research designed to show that "complementary and alternative" medical treatments (such as acupuncture, meditation, and prayer) have demonstrably positive effects on health. While its objectives have evolved, it still funds research for treatments based on cultural beliefs.

It is fair to say that this research has not greatly altered the practice of medicine in America. Faith in alternative medical treatments does not arise from, nor is it based on, an understanding of science; so further scientific research is not likely to enhance or diminish belief in these interventions. Perhaps the most salient finding from this research is evidence that patients in placebo control groups experience significant benefits. The effectiveness of placebos in relieving symptoms of medical disorders has apparently increased in recent years, suggesting that credulity and self-delusion are increasing.

Delusions

Delusions are personal systems of belief that are not shared by the greater community. The belief that we can control events with our thoughts is considered delusional in most cultures, but the belief that events can be influenced by prayer is seen by many as a truth validated by sacred revelations and personal experience.

In many cultures, belief in conspiracy theories is so common that it is not considered delusional. Many people around the world have expressed a belief that the CIA arranged to have airplanes flown into the World Trade Center in New York City on September 11, 2001. This belief is so widespread in some Islamic societies that it is not considered a delusion or even a theory, but a known fact.

Paranoid delusions of grandeur or persecution may find a home in ordinary people. Some of us, at times, accept popular conspiracy theories, even though we may recoil instinctively when a wide-eyed stranger tells us that the videos of the moon landings were staged in a studio in California. We may say the fellow is "in his own little world," or label him a "nut case," but we may hesitate to use stronger language, or to be more specific, lest we offend a listener who holds equally exotic beliefs.

Paranoid delusions may lie just beneath the surface of a normal personality. Otherwise-normal people may attempt to control events with their thoughts and wishes, or may believe that their colleagues are conspiring against them. So long as their level of paranoia remains more-or-less representative of their culture, they can go through life without being labeled psychotic, but there are limits to what societies will tolerate. In the case of paranoid delusions, that limit usually occurs when others begin to feel physically threatened.

A delusional person with a charismatic personality may develop a cult of followers to share and support those delusions. In the case of the 1978 Jonestown massacre in Guyana, American minister Jim Jones ordered the murder/suicide of his 913 Christian followers. In 1997 in Rancho Santa Fe, California, thirty-nine members of the Heaven's Gate cult, followers of Marshall Applewhite and Bonnie Lu Nettles, committed suicide. They reportedly believed that by committing suicide in a timely fashion, they would ascend to rendezvous with a spaceship following closely behind the Hale-Bopp Comet that was approaching Earth.

Because their belief system did not conform to any widely held religious beliefs, cult leaders as well as the people who believed their teachings could have been diagnosed as psychotic. But to their followers, these leaders were not suffering paranoid delusions but were visionaries in possession of rare truths.

Political Ideologies

Political ideologies that cannot be safely questioned or doubted also fall within the domain of Mystica. The landscape of the United States and other countries is dotted with communities established as utopian societies. I live in a small town developed over a century ago as an experimental colony dedicated to the single-tax economic tenets of Henry George, author of *Progress and Poverty* (1880). When these "single taxers" from Iowa reached the eastern shore of Mobile Bay in the 1890s, the existing residents must have viewed them with suspicion and considered them and their economic beliefs to be cultish. But cult or not, the utopian colony eventually became an influential part of the larger community.

Both political and religious faiths teach that assertions are false if they are not in accord with their doctrinal teachings and revelations. Nationalistic ideologies such as communism, fascism, Nazism, and other authoritarian forms of government require a personal commitment to doctrines and leaders. Political ideologies may, like religious scriptures, promise deliverance, but that deliverance is material rather than spiritual.

Communistic doctrines, promoted a century ago by revolutionaries inside the Kremlin, rejected all religious faiths and required Russian citizens to live their lives in accordance with the teachings of Karl Marx and Vladimir Lenin, communism's chief prophets. After his death, Lenin's Tomb attracted pilgrims just as a religious shrine would. Similarly, Adolph Hitler's hold over the German people was not unlike that of a religious prophet. He identified the forces allied against the Aryan "race" and set forth steps to overcome these forces. He dealt harshly with nonbelievers who rejected his message or failed to show fealty. Hitler was both a prophet and a martyred leader to people who believed (or still believe) in the genetic superiority of "white" people.

The Emotional Domain

In comparison to the other three domains, Mystica's truths are held with an emotional fervor. Spiritual leaders play on emotions with dramatic and elaborate ceremonies, rituals, music, icons, and edifices designed to inspire reverence, fear, love, ecstasy, contentment, or other feelings. Primitive holy men evoked feelings of awe with displays of magic, and some evangelical ministers play on the fears of their audiences with threats of a vividly-described hell and eternal suffering. Believers often interpret their emotional reactions as validation of the truth of the message, and may be overcome with emotions when testifying about their faith.

When we meet people who ask about our religious or political affiliations, we may be reluctant to say much because we don't know what their reaction might be. At family or social gatherings, we may refuse to discuss religious beliefs or political ideologies, in order to avoid creating an unpleasant emotional scene.

Disputes about truths in the other three domains can also become emotional, but generally, people are quite tolerant or even indifferent to attacks on or ridicule of their opinions, logical inferences, and reports of research findings. Beliefs, however, are different. We tend to have strong feelings about our beliefs, and we want others to respect those feelings.

In many religions, taboo words or profane assertions may provoke anger and lead to threats. Humorous representations or criticisms of the Prophet Mohammed have led to the issuance of fatwas (death orders). The British author Salman Rushdie spent years avoiding public appearances after his 1988 novel *The Satanic Verses* made him the target of a fatwa issued by Ayatollah Khomeini.

Faith, War, and Terror

The path to war often runs through Mystica, where truths, stated absolutely, stir passions and fears. The disputes that lead to war and terrorism are seldom about popular opinions, logical proofs, or research findings, but they do often arise from religious disagreements or conflicting political ideologies, and they may be exacerbated by greed, racism, power struggles, fear, and militancy.

The stark moral contrasts that religious and ideological leaders paint between good (or superior) and evil (or inferior) prepares like-minded believers to fight wars against people who do not share their beliefs. Whether it is Christians on crusades, Nazis exterminating Jews, communists banning religion, or militant jihadists terrorizing infidels, the predisposing factor is much the same: the faithful are guided and motivated by their possession of absolute and final truths.

Of course, war is possible without Mystica's truths, but the certainty and passion of faith provide a natural pathway to war. We can find wars fought between nations with shared political and religious ideologies, where the dispute is a matter of border location, conquest, or retribution. But soldiers are always more willing to kill those who are defending a different faith or a repugnant political ideology.

Across the decades of the Cold War, the American government faced few difficulties in motivating soldiers and civilians alike to prepare for war against "atheistic communists." After all, communists opposed the core values and beliefs commonly advocated in the United States: individual freedom, democracy, capitalism, and faith in God.

*   *   *   *   *

In spite of its threat to peace, Mystica will always provide one of the four paths to truth, so it is important that this emotional domain be understood, managed, and contained. When a society of believers indoctrinates its children to hate inferiors, enemies, infidels, or heretics, the seeds of conflict are planted, and the problem can grow unmanageable as these children mature.

Eighty years ago, European democracies faced war against soldiers who, as children, were indoctrinated in Nazi and Fascist ideologies. Today the threat of war against democracies comes from people who grew up being told that Jews and Christians are their enemies. Some Jewish and Christian fundamentalists, in turn, teach their children that Muslims are their mortal enemy. Mystica offers a path to truths of faith, but not necessarily a path to peaceful coexistence.

4

Logica: The Land of Reason

LOGICA'S TRUTHS MUST pass the tests of reason—that is, they must be logically proven to be true. A truth from the domain of Logica can be discredited only by showing that it was illogically inferred, or that it was based on a false premise.

In most decisions, we can rely on common sense derived from personal experience, but when we encounter situations or questions that require precise and reliable answers—such as making travel arrangements for a long trip, or calculating the lowest cost per ounce for products that come in multiple sizes—we must resort to logical analysis.

We tend to develop either a personal aversion to or an affinity for logical analysis. Those of us who are comfortable solving logical problems are often attracted to engineering, medicine, accounting, and other professions that require careful analysis of facts and logically valid inferences from those facts. Societies hold members of these rational professions in high regard and pay them well, but because faulty reasoning can result in devastating harm, such professionals may be held liable for their errors in reasoning.

Logical Reasoning

When people with poor reasoning skills encounter problems that require logical analysis, they may look for a quick and easy way out, offering personal opinions or flippant guesses, or treating the problem as a word game or riddle. People who routinely deal with logical problems are usually reluctant to hazard opinions or guesses; they want time to analyze the problem and find a logical answer.

In 1966 cognitive psychologist Peter C. Wason designed a logical task to study "confirmation bias," that is, our tendency to look for evidence that supports our bias, rather than looking for ways to refute it. The following adaptation of Wason's Selection Task will allow you to explore your critical thinking skills. You can decide on your answer, and then read on.

Given: Four cards are displayed on a table. Each card has a circle on one side and a square on other side.

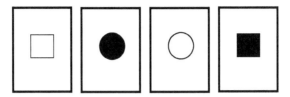

Question: Which card or cards must be turned over to test the truth of the following assertion: *Each card with a white square on one side has a black circle on the other side.*

Only by carefully reasoned analysis are you likely to find the right answer to this question. People who are uncomfortable with logical problems may find the question frustrating or uninteresting, but people who take pride in their reasoning skills will likely find the question engaging, and *if they are cautious* they can find the correct answer.

The first step is to analyze the problem and frame the question in a simpler way. Here is the question as originally stated:

Which card or cards must be turned over to test the truth of the following assertion? *Each card with a white square on one side has a black circle on the other side.*

We can restate the question in a clearer way:

How can we be certain that no card with a white square on one side has a white circle on the other side?

Now, with the question restated, the problem is all but solved; the next step is to recognize that only the cards showing a white square or a white circle can refute the assertion. For the purpose of answering the original question, the other two cards do not matter—that is, regardless of what is on the other side, they cannot possibly refute the assertion being tested.

Dialectical vs. Rhetorical Argument

The search for reasoned truth often takes the form of a rational discourse that considers the pros and cons of a problem—that is, a *dialectical* discussion. The objective of participants in a dialectical conversation is to raise questions and to search for factual and logical answers. For example, when detectives discuss a murder case, they may first ask, "What do we know?" Once they have thoroughly researched all the available evidence and generated a list of facts and suspects, they may then ask, "What can we logically conclude from what we know?"

Dialectical arguments are similar to rhetorical arguments, but the participants have different objectives. In a dialectical discussion the objective is to discover the truth by asking questions, ascertaining facts, and drawing valid conclusions from the facts, whereas in a rhetorical argument the objective is to persuade others and to win an argument. The detectives in the above example seek the truth, but the attorneys who prosecute or defend the accused are only trying to persuade the jurors, so finding the truth is not their objective, although they may stoutly maintain that it is.

Formal Arguments: The Syllogism

We can find reasoned truth through dialectical discourse, but we can also find truth through the methods of formal logic. To readers who might be put off by the demands of formal logic, let me assure you that we are not going far with this topic. We will focus on simple arguments and employ the intuitive approach to examine common errors in reasoning.

Let's begin by reviewing a basic reasoning procedure called the *syllogism*. In a three-part syllogism, two premises are given, and a conclusion is logically inferred or deduced from those premises. Each of the three propositions specifies quantity (for example, *all* or *some*), and each has a linking verb (such as *is* or *are*) connecting the subject and predicate. Consider the following syllogism:

> PREMISE 1: All human beings are mortal.
> PREMISE 2: All Italians are human beings.
> CONCLUSION: Therefore, all Italians are mortal.

The truth of the conclusion depends not only on the truth of the two premises but also on the validity of the reasoning. Three questions must be raised to evaluate the truth of the conclusion: Is Premise 1 true? Is Premise 2 true? And can the conclusion be logically inferred from the two premises? If you decide the answer to all three questions is "yes," then you must accept the conclusion as true. If you cannot intuitively decide whether the conclusion is logically inferred from the premises, ask yourself the question: Is there any way both premises can be true without the conclusion also being true? Since the answer in the case of our example is *no*, you can see that the conclusion was validly inferred.

The logical implications of a syllogism extend beyond the stated conclusion. Each of the three propositions may contradict or agree with other propositions that are not part of this specific syllogism. For example: If it is true that *all* Italians are mortal, then it would be contradictory also to state that *some* Italians are immortal. And, if all Italians are mortal, then certainly we can say that *any specific* Italian is mortal.

Premises may be true by definition, they may be intuitively true, or they may be inferred from some previous reasoning, or they may simply be stipulated as true for the sake of argument. Consider the following examples:

> TRUE BY DEFINITION: All triangles have three sides.
> INTUITIVELY TRUE: No part is greater than the whole.
> REASONED TRUTH: All Italians are mortal (conclusion of the syllogism above).
> STIPULATED AS TRUE: All human behavior is predictable.

Regardless of the type of premises involved, the truth of the conclusion of a three-part syllogism always depends upon both premises being true.

Formal logic may seem irrelevant to the individual who relies on *common sense*. My first college algebra course began with a logical proof that methods of addition always yielded the correct answer. As a college freshman with the usual store of common sense, I failed to see any need for such a proof. I was willing to accept without question that the rules of mathematics, addition included, always worked flawlessly. But my professor followed the methods of Logica and gave us a proof; for him, mathematical operations had to be validated logically, regardless of how much they appealed to, or contradicted, common sense.

Errors in Reasoning

The rules of Logica can be difficult to follow, causing people to make logical errors that lead them away from truth. Common flaws in the logic used in rhetorical arguments were presented in Chapter Two, and here we will look at some common logical errors that occur when we engage in a rational search for truth.

Presuming Causation

Consider the following argument:

> There is a positive correlation between education and income; therefore, higher levels of education lead to higher incomes.

We can see the problem with the conclusion by looking at alternative explanations for the correlation. For example, people with greater motivation and focus tend to succeed both in school and at work. In that case, educational and financial success would be correlated not because one causes the other, but because they have a common cause. Just because an event precedes a correlated event, it cannot be assumed to have caused that event. This common type of logical error is labeled a *post hoc ergo propter hoc* (after this, therefore on account of this) argument.

Tautological Explanations

Perhaps the most common illogical statement is the tautological explanation, in which *A* is presented as the cause (or explanation) of *A-identified-by-another-name.* For example, consider this statement: "He breaks the law because he is a criminal." This meaningless account offers a label, "criminal," as an explanation of crime. On analysis, we can see that the explanation says only that *he breaks the law because he is a lawbreaker,* a meaningless non-explanation.

Even in academic settings, where teachers are dedicated to following the rules of reason, tautological explanations are still common. Here are four representative examples:

> He learns fast because he is a *bright* student.
> The economy is performing poorly because we are
> in a *recession.*
> Objects are pulled toward the earth by *gravity.*
> *Bipolar disorders* cause extreme mood swings.

With careful analysis, we see that these examples actually explain nothing. Each presents a label or name as an explanation or cause. Each amounts to no more than saying "A is the cause of A," which is nonsense.

Affirming the Consequent

People frequently commit the logical fallacy of affirming the consequent. Consider the following if/then reasoning:

> If it rains, then the ground will be wet.
> We find the ground wet.
> We conclude that it has rained.

But affirming that the ground is wet (the consequent) does not establish that it has rained (the antecedent). At best, we can assert that it may have rained, but it is certainly possible that something else—a sprinkler, or a leaking water main, for instance—caused the ground to be wet. Put symbolically, "If A then B" does not imply the reverse: "If B then A."

Commonsense Bias

All of us suffer from a tendency to accept any line of reasoning that reaches a conclusion that appeals to our biases or common sense. Consider the syllogism below:

> PREMISE 1: All birds are animals.
> PREMISE 2: All ducks are animals.
> CONCLUSION: Therefore, all ducks are birds.

Because the conclusion appears true on its face, we tend to assume that the reasoning is valid. But in this case the conclusion does not follow from the premises, and therefore the argument is not valid. Note: We are not saying the conclusion is false—ducks are in fact birds—but that particular conclusion cannot be logically inferred from the two premises given, even though the premises are also true. Study the syllogism and attempt to determine what's wrong with the reasoning. The syllogism would have been valid if it were changed to read as follows:

> PREMISE 1: All birds are animals.
> PREMISE 2: All ducks are birds.
> CONCLUSION: Therefore, all ducks are animals.

The argument below reaches a conclusion that is contrary to common sense, at least for Americans:

> PREMISE 1: All mortals are liars.
> PREMISE 2: All Americans are mortals.
> CONCLUSION: Therefore, all Americans are liars.

The tendency might be for Americans to disagree with the conclusion, and therefore to assert that the argument is not valid, although it is. Read the syllogism carefully and you will see that the conclusion follows logically from the premises. And if you accept both premises, you must then accept the conclusion.

The three-part syllogisms above are among the simplest formal arguments. As arguments become more complex, we may find it far more difficult to discover logical flaws. If we depend on common sense, we are destined to accept many false arguments, and to reject many valid arguments. Only by mastering the formal rules of logic can we avoid errors in reasoning and overcome our commonsense biases.

History of Logica

Evidence for the existence of sound logical reasoning is found thousands of years ago, with the first calendars and geometric constructions. The design and construction of Egyptian pyramids, over four thousand years ago, required precise reasoning. But the development of Logica's formal methods for validation of the truth of propositions came much later.

The Golden Age of Greece: 500-300 BCE

The formal foundation of Logica can be traced to the Golden Age of Greece. The nineteenth-century German scholar Eduard Zeller said (see *Outlines of The History of Greek Philosophy, 13th Edition,* 1980): "Never did a people judge its own nature and the institutions, morals and customs which it produced with greater impartiality than the Greeks." From Thales to Xenophanes, Pythagorus, Heraclitus, Parmenides, Anaxagorus, and Empedocles, the pre-Socratic Greek philosophers relied on reasoning to solve the mysteries of the cosmos, and of life itself.

Few pre-Socratics trusted reason more than did Parmenides, a politician who retired to study philosophy. Zeller summarizes one of Parmenides' teachings in the following way:

> The only perception which is true is that which shows us in everything an unchanging Being, namely Reason (λογος); the senses, on the other hand, which present to us a manifold of things, creation, destruction and change, that is a being of Not-Being, are the cause of all error.

Parmenides' trust in reason exceeded his trust in his own perceptions, a theme that recurred in the teachings of Plato and other Greek philosophers.

But not all Greek scholars placed complete trust in logical reasoning. For a time, Greek teachers known as sophists (specifically, Protagoras and his followers) made rhetorical attacks on reason, identifying common sense and popular opinion as more trustworthy, but the domain of

Logica survived the sophists, and for centuries its influence continued to expand in the small world of Greek scholars and teachers.

While most modern scholars embraced the truths of logic, ordinary people, as well as political and religious leaders, often rejected them. Then as now, ordinary citizens fear unrestrained reason when it questions popular opinions and beliefs. They remain on the side of the sophists, trusting the truths of Rhetorica and Mystica when they conflict with the truths of reason.

When the Greek scholar Socrates taught his students to question popular opinions and beliefs, he was accused of corrupting the youth of Athens. His teachings may have passed Logica's test but they failed to obtain cultural endorsements. Socrates was charged, tried, and condemned to death. He left no written record of his teachings, but they would live on in the works of his student Plato.

Plato's analyses of topics such as physics, ethics, politics, art, and religion gave new stature to the rational search for truth, and Plato's student Aristotle advanced the standing of Logica even further by developing the formal methods of deductive and inductive reasoning still taught today.

Aristotle employed intuitive or axiomatic truth to establish premises from which his reasoning could start. He stated in *Posterior Analytics*: "...since except intuition nothing can be truer than scientific knowledge, it will be intuition that apprehends the primary premises...." He accepted self-evident or intuitive truths without the need for proof or challenge. As an example of intuitive truth, we might select Euclid's Fifth Axiom, which states that only one parallel line (of any set of parallel lines) can be drawn through a given point. Euclid asserted his geometric axioms as true because they were self-evident, that is, obvious and certain, and logically valid theorems derived from these axioms would also be accepted as certain.

Logica in the Dark Ages

With the death of Alexander the Great in 323 BCE, the Greek Empire began a long decline, and the center of political and military power gradually shifted from Greece to Rome. While Greek and Roman scholars continued the search for truth through reason, most citizens still sought the blessing and guidance of their gods and goddesses.

Romans who could afford the considerable costs joined cults associated with specific gods—for example, the cult of Mithras or the cult of Isis. The most successful cult, however, was the Jesus movement. Although the movement originated as a small Hebrew cult, it grew rapidly after Paul of Tarsus invited Romans of all classes to join and follow the teachings of Jesus.

By refusing to pay homage to the Roman gods, members of the Jesus movement at first amused, and later plagued, Roman emperors. Even more troubling to Rome was the fact that these followers of Jesus, known as *believers,* continued to attract new followers, spreading their influence across the Empire. In 380 Emperor Theodosius I made Christianity the state religion of the Empire, thereby reconciling Roman law with the growing Christian community.

Over the coming century, the Roman Empire declined as the Roman Church gained political power. Christianity would grow to exert control over Western thought for nearly a thousand years. This period, in which the Roman Church suppressed the search for truth in Logica, is now referred to as the Dark Ages. All across Christendom many of the teachings of Greek philosophers were lost or deliberately destroyed. Fortunately for the domain of Logica, the Greek Empire had once extended into North Africa, and many writings from the Golden Age of Greece were kept in the library at Alexandria. When the city fell to Muslim Arabs in 641 these writings were preserved and then at the end of the Dark Ages rediscovered by Christians.

Logica's Renaissance

Sixteen hundred years after Aristotle's death, and a millennium after the Roman Empire's acceptance of Christianity, the door opened for the Christian rediscovery of Greek philosophy. At the request of colleagues, William of Moerbeke (c. 1215–1286), the Flemish-born Bishop of Corinth, took on the task of translating several philosophical, scientific, and medical works from original Greek to Latin, the language of the Church. His translations gave Thomas Aquinas, an influential Italian priest and friend of Moerbeke, access to the writings of Aristotle. Thomas reconciled Aristotle's logical teachings with Christian theology by arguing that truth is conceived and tested by the mind, but he still allowed the search for truth to be open to divine revelation.

With the resurgence of trust in human reasoning, the authority of the Church of Rome was increasingly questioned. During the sixteenth century, Martin Luther, a priest and professor of theology, disputed the Church's claim that God's punishment of sin could be avoided through the purchase of indulgences. With the apocryphal posting of his Ninety-Five Theses on the door of the Wittenberg Castle Church, Martin Luther openly challenged the authority of Rome and ignited a theological rebellion that culminated in the Protestant Reformation. As the authority of the Church of Rome waned, logical reasoning slowly regained its hold on Western thought, and many scholars and thinkers openly turned to the methods of Logica in their search for truth.

The Age of Reason

By offering rational explanations of human nature and God's Universe, the seventeenth-century English Philosopher Thomas Hobbes challenged the teachings of the Christian Church in particular, and the truths of Mystica in general. Hobbes argued that all of nature, man and politics included, is mechanistic, and thus open to rational understanding. His respect for reasoned truth is illustrated in his explanation of *difference*, which appeared in his *Elements of Philosophy (1655)*:

> Two bodies are said to differ from one another, when something may be said of one of them, which cannot be said of the other at the same time. And, first of all, it is manifest that no two bodies are the same: for seeing they are two, they are in two places at the same time; as that, which is the same, is at the same time in one and the same place.

For most thinkers, the definition of *difference* could be left to common usage and common sense, but for Hobbes it required a clarification that only logical analysis could provide.

In the seventeenth and eighteenth centuries, empiricists such as John Locke, James Berkeley, and David Hume described the development of the mind as a natural process. They explained knowledge and understanding as products of sensory experience. In the nineteenth century, the associationists James Mills, John Stuart Mills, and Herbert Spencer went further, describing learning and thinking as associative processes of the mind.

In the Western world, as Christian monarchs began to accommodate democratic institutions of government, more scholars began to challenge the truths of Christianity, and universities promoted respect for secular reasoning in a manner not seen since the Golden Age of Greece. Philosophers continued to advance the truths of reason, and books on philosophy were increasingly available. With the growing dissemination of reasoned truths, the status of Logica continued to rise in the Western World, gradually displacing Mystica as the primary domain of truth, at least among the well educated.

Academia

Over the first half of the nineteenth century, Western colleges broke free from the restraints of religion by openly embracing the methods of reason. Colleges grew as forums for, and in tribute to, the truths of reason, becoming subcultures where Logica's elders could freely pursue and defend their truths. Logical analysis became the academic test of truth.

Educated Western students mastered not only Latin, the language of the Roman Church, but also Greek, the language of Plato and Aristotle. Students were also free to study the secular philosophy of British empiricists as well as the mathematical truths advanced by Descartes, Newton, and Leibniz. The uneducated masses remained under the sway of the revealed truths of religion; and the educated class, especially in England, thought it unwise to share their religious skepticism with people of the working classes.

The last half of the nineteenth century saw a trend toward dividing areas of philosophical inquiry into academic departments. Philosophy branched into new disciplines of science and humanities, even though the highest academic degree in each remained the Doctor of Philosophy, and all scholars were expected to master the methods of logical reasoning.

In the twentieth century, professors across a wide array of academic disciplines relied on the rules of logic to organize their subject matter and to engage their students in dialectical discussions, but in the last half of the twentieth century higher education became available to an ever-increasing range of students. Logica saw its status decline as teachers found it increasingly difficult to be faithful to the rules of reason. Many students were not able to follow well-reasoned arguments, and many teachers mitigated their insistence on rigorous reasoning. Students were increasingly allowed to express personal opinions and to engage in rhetorical debate.

Hard-won academic freedoms that once permitted teachers and students to pursue the rational truths of their discipline, free from governmental control and the influence of religion, are still prized but little understood. The original purpose of academic freedom had been turned on its head and reconceived as a license to escape the restraints of logic and promote personal beliefs and political ideologies.

In modern American dramas, professors and scholars are often portrayed as ideological zealots vigorously defending opinions and promoting their beliefs. To the extent that this caricature of academic life reflects reality in the slightest, schools have failed to remain faithful to their domain of truth, and have faltered in their defense and promotion of the methods and truths of Logica.

5

Empirica: The Land of Reality

RESEARCH IS A slow, dirty-hands approach to truth. In every scientific discipline, assertions of truth must be based on rigorous and time-consuming research. Astronomers study the universe by collecting and analyzing voluminous quantities of data on the forms and movements of celestial bodies. Geologists trace physical history by collecting and analyzing data from layers of the earth, and anthropologists collect and classify remains, artifacts, and records surviving from ancient human cultures.

There are no safe shortcuts along the path to factual understanding. In Empirica, no theory, regardless of how widely acknowledged or logical it may be, is accepted as true unless supportive data are provided, and each new theory must survive research designed purposefully to reveal its flaws.

Empirica's Methods

While technological advances (e.g., clocks, compasses, telescopes, microscopes, cameras, x-ray, spectrometers, particle accelerators, and magnetic resonance imaging) make new discoveries possible, it is the methods of empirical research, rather than the technology used, that establish which assertions and theoretical accounts should be accepted as true.

The three general categories of research methods are: field studies, correlational studies, and experiments. *Field studies* involve systematic observation and recording of events and processes. Researchers armed with notebooks, check sheets, charts, cameras, telescopes, and recording devices, document their observations of life, objects, and events. Since ancient times, astronomers have charted the night sky, looking for patterns. Today, a botanist might record the types and numbers of plants observed in a remote river delta, and a sociologist might set up an observation post in a shopping mall, from which to observe and record the frequency and form of social interactions among shoppers. Findings from such field studies provide descriptions of phenomena, events, and processes, and these findings, in turn, can generate hypotheses about the relationships among variables. The truth of such hypothesized relationships can then be tested in correlational studies or experiments.

Correlational studies involve the collection of specific data pairs to assess the degree and direction of the relationship between variables. For example, income and education level might be measured for a large number of randomly selected individuals; the degree to which income is related to education can then be calculated mathematically. If incomes tend to be higher among people with higher levels of education, the correlation is positive; but if higher incomes are linked to lower education levels, then a negative correlation, or inverse relationship, exists. A strong correlation, either positive or negative, allows us to estimate with confidence the value of one variable from known values of the other. That is, for any person income can be estimated from education, or education can be estimated from income. The accuracy of such estimates will always depend on the degree of correlation, not the direction of the relationship between the two variables.

Regardless of the direction or degree of the relationship, we cannot conclude from a correlational study that changes in one variable will produce a change in the other. That is, we cannot state that more education improves income or that more income improves education. Only an experiment can tell us whether or not there is a causal relationship.

An *experiment* requires manipulation of a hypothesized cause and the measurement of subsequent changes in the hypothesized effect. For example, a researcher might hypothesize that preschool education improves performance in the first grade. To evaluate this claim, the researcher might randomly divide a group of four-year-olds into two classes. One class would receive preschool education while the other class, known as the "control group," is allowed to play games. If children who receive preschool education perform significantly better in the first grade than do the children from the control group, the researcher can say with some confidence that preschool education *produced or caused* that improvement. The researcher must, however, insure that no other differences in treatment or selection of the two groups could account for the difference, and must also mathematically calculate the probability that the observed improvement could have occurred as a result of chance variation in the make-up of the groups. Only when observed improvements are quite unlikely to have occurred by chance (generally a 5% or less probability of occurring by chance) will the findings be accepted as trustworthy and labeled "significant."

The three research methods—field studies, correlational studies, and experiments—were devised to test and establish the truth about the occurrence and relationships among variables. Field studies can test the truth of assertions about the rate of occurrence of objects and events, correlation studies can test the truth of assertions about the degree and direction of relationships, and experiments can test hypotheses about cause and effect.

Any factual assertion or theoretical explanation that passes the appropriate test of rigorous research can be listed among the truths of Empirica. In the domain of Empirica, however, truths are subject to revision. They can be questioned and re-tested in future research, and must pass all new research-based tests to which they are subjected.

Basic vs. Applied Science

Prior to World War II, scientific research was largely focused on establishing the basic truths of nature. Researchers sought answers to questions such as: What is light? How did the universe form? When did humans evolve? What are the processes of the brain? What is the nature of perception? The mandate for researchers was to answer the fundamental questions about nature. The search for facts relevant to daily life was seen as less important in the advancement of understanding. Anyone who asked what difference basic research findings would make in our daily lives might have received a short answer, "We don't know."

But in the can-do, consumer-driven era that followed World War II, the cultural mandate for research changed. Everyone knew that scientific research could solve human problems, and people began to presume that was the justification for, and perhaps the purpose of, all scientific research. The social mandate shifted more toward the practical needs of society, like finding cures for illnesses, or creating new technologies for military defense. By the end of the 1960s, research just for the sake of discovering basic truths about nature had become increasingly difficult to fund.

In America medical and military research programs absorbed billions of dollars in governmental funding each year, while basic research operated on a tighter budget. In the United States in 2010, the total budget granted for basic research by the National Science Foundation was seven billion dollars. In comparison, the National Institute of Health received thirty billion dollars, and the Department of Defense budgeted seventy-nine billion dollars for research. Major universities became increasingly interested in promoting applied research as a means for obtaining large research grants.

Funding for applied science came not only from governmental sources but also from businesses with a financial interest in research outcomes. Researchers who reported that products were safe and effective might find manufacturers more willing to fund further research, or willing to show their appreciation in other ways. Obviously, such rewards constituted a conflict of interest, and nowhere was the conflict more evident than in drug research. Pharmaceutical companies fund research on their products, and stand to make billions of dollars in profits when new products are found to be safe and effective, whereas a single negative research report may result in a drug being pulled from the market, costing the manufacturer dearly.

Since the 1960s, drug companies promoted the view that psychiatric problems are caused by chemical imbalances in the brain. Anti-psychotic, anti-anxiety, and anti-depressant drugs have been developed to "correct those imbalances," but the original claim, that mental problems result from chemical imbalance, has never been established. In fact, some of these drugs may cause side effects because they actually *create* chemical imbalances in the body.

Only when there is a barrier between researchers and their funding sources can the integrity of applied research be assured, and only then should the findings be seen as factually true. When drug companies provide researchers with research grants, appointments to boards, speaking fees, gifts or awards, or travel funds, we should not associate those researchers' findings with the term *science*, applied or otherwise. It is commercial research that should be labeled product research and development (i.e., R & D).

Facts of History

Both science and history establish factual truths, but they differ in their social relevance. Science focuses our attention on possibilities for the future while history anchors us with realities of the past. We value science for the ability it gives us to predict and control future events and to develop new technologies, while history's primary value is the context it provides for understanding and interpreting cultural, technical, economic, and political changes. Both fields discover facts through research, and both help us understand reality.

Even though science and history occupy different niches in the traditional college curriculum, they search for truth in the same domain. Both are founded on the methods of systematic data collection, empirical descriptions, and precise documentation of findings. Just as geologists document the where, when, and how of *physical* history, historians document the where, when, and how of *human* history.

Governments and churches have for centuries kept written records, maps, and paintings, but in the twentieth century, history became more objective and academic, and moved away from the political and religious perspectives and influences. Modern methods of research and documentation have allowed many earlier historical accounts to be re-analyzed and revised. Egyptian mummies were subjected to electronic imaging studies, cargo from ancient shipwrecks was retrieved and analyzed, and DNA technology allowed kinship analysis of prominent historical families.

More facts of human history were recorded and documented during the twentieth century than had been amassed in all previous human existence. Cameras, recorders, copiers, and, more recently, digital media have made it possible to preserve historical events in ways unimaginable in earlier times. Future historians will have huge quantities of material to mine for facts that go unrecognized today.

Theory or Fact?

In popular parlance, the word *theory* suggests speculation and the word *fact* suggests certainty. Like many dichotomies, this is an artificial dissection of what is actually a continuum. Along this continuum, the more general, explanatory, and untested an assertion is, the more likely it is to be called a *theory*, whereas more specific, descriptive, and established assertions are likely to be called *facts*. Is it a theory that smoking increases the probability of lung cancer, or is it a fact? Is global warming theory or fact? Is it theory or fact that Lee Harvey Oswald killed President Kennedy? To be accepted in Empirica, all assertions about reality, whether called *theory* or *fact*, must be based on, and consistent with, relevant research findings.

For rhetorical purposes, an inconvenient fact is sometimes demeaned as "just a theory." One recently occurring example involves the assertion by Christian fundamentalists that evolution is "just a theory." But evolution is not a theory; it is a fact. The vast array of fossils and bones discovered, dated, and documented, shows that life forms changed slowly, or *evolved*, over millions of years—those are the facts. Several theories have been proposed to account for this evolution of life forms, ranging from Jean-Baptiste Lamarck's theory of inheritance of acquired characteristics to Charles Darwin's theory of natural selection to Herbert Spencer's "survival of the fittest" to modern theories based on improved understanding of genetics and sociobiology. But as new theories of evolution are proposed, tested, and refined or discarded, documented research findings continue to confirm the fact that all species (human beings included) evolved.

Scientists are reluctant to propose speculative theories about what *might* be the case; rather, they theorize cautiously, driven by the need to unify research findings. They use logic to develop theories and to design experimental tests of those theories, but it is the data, the findings of the experiments, that determine the fate of the theories.

Unexplained data push scientists toward new theories. In reporting data on the bones he collected and the species he observed, Charles Darwin noted that life on the Galapagos Archipelago had evolved over time, and later proposed his theory of natural selection—but with great reluctance, in part because of the public criticism he anticipated.

Theorists who reason ahead of the data do so at great professional risk. Only a few theorists, Albert Einstein being one of the most notable examples, have successfully reasoned far ahead of available data. When such speculative theorizing succeeds and produces an explanation that passes the test of research to become established as true, the story may be highly publicized and incorrectly presented as typical science.

Regardless of how logical such speculative theories may appear, when they are tested empirically they usually die quick deaths. As a general rule, successful theorists remain in close contact with their subject matter, and let research data drive their theorizing. We admire Einstein's intellect because he broke the rule of caution and succeeded, taking physics forward in a giant leap, but many equally intelligent researchers have developed speculative theories of nature that were just as well reasoned, but wrong nonetheless.

Empirica's Truth

No other domain can rival Empirica's progress in the twentieth century, but in no domain is the word *truth* less welcome. To researchers, *truth* sounds too final, too certain, to be applied to research conclusions that can be discarded or revised as a result of future findings.

Contrary to conventional understanding, research can never *prove* the truth of an assertion of fact—it can only *support* the assertion. As the theoretical physicist Richard Feynman said in *The Relation of Science and Religion* (1956):

> "...as you develop more information in the sciences, it is not that you are finding out the truth, but that you are finding out that this or that is more or less likely."

The researcher's task is never to *prove* a theory, but to conduct research that can potentially *refute* a theory. Previous research support, regardless of how abundant and prestigious it may be, pales in comparison to one new experimental test that the theory fails. On the other hand, each time a theory passes an exacting new experimental test, greater confidence is placed in it. The more demanding and precise the test, the more confidence increases. But regardless of the level of confidence researchers have in their facts and theories, Empirica's "truths" are never proven. The word *proof* should be reserved for use in Logica.

Un-testable Theories

A scientific theory must be testable and, to be accepted as true, it must pass the tests of empirical research. If a theory cannot predict measurable outcomes, it cannot be tested, and therefore cannot be refuted (or supported) by research findings. Such un-testable theories must be discarded and ignored in Empirica.

Un-testable theories often persist in the popular literature precisely *because* no conceivable research finding can refute them. For example, neither Freudian theory nor the theory of intelligent design emerged as a product of research findings, and no experiment has been designed to potentially refute either. Try to imagine the research outcome that would show that psychological decisions do not result from a struggle among three invisible and inscrutable mental forces—id, ego, and superego. And what research finding could demonstrate that the order found in nature is not "intelligent"? Freudian theory and intelligent design theory survive because they were tested and confirmed in accordance with the rules of Rhetorica and Mystica, respectively, not the rules of Empirica.

Science and Reason

Science is frequently, but incorrectly, described as the rational pursuit of truth. Scientists can be quite rational in constructing theories and designing research projects to answer empirical questions, but regardless of the level of reasoning that goes into theorizing, research design, and data analysis, it is recorded data that test and establish the facts of Empirica.

Researchers generally abide by the rules of reason when they construct theories, but in Empirica a new theory is not presumed to be true just because it is logical. To be accepted in Empirica, a theory must be shown to accurately predict research findings.

In 1943, Clarke L. Hull, a distinguished experimental psychologist affiliated with Yale University, developed a logical and elegant theory of learning. The theory can be summarized in common terms as stating that performance can be predicted by multiplying units of motivation by units of learning. Unfortunately, his well-reasoned and mathematically precise theory did not withstand the tests of research that it invited, and his theory of learning was eventually transferred to the dustbins of history, a victim of research findings.

Reason has often led scientists down blind alleys. For example, in the nineteenth century, physicists understood that waves could only occur in a medium; for example, sound waves can occur in air, in water, or in other substances, but they cannot pass through a vacuum. When it was discovered that light also moves in waves, the question arose: "What is the medium?" Since light waves can pass through a vacuum, reason suggested that a vacuum must contain some medium to convey the waves. Physicists named this invisible medium the *luminiferous aether*. Even though the logical necessity of the aether seemed compelling, research never revealed the existence of any such substance. When the findings of Albert Michelson and

Edward Morley's famous experiment in 1887 failed to support the luminiferous aether theory, physicists reluctantly began to accept the fact that light waves occur without a medium—even though this fact appeared then, and still appears, to be unreasonable. Reason still asks, "Waves in what?"

Nineteenth century experimental psychologists fell victim to similar reasoning, when they observed and documented how people are changed by experience. This fact led them to accept the notion that psychological experiences produce *things*—images, ideas, and memories—that are stored inside the person, in a psychological aether called the *mind*. Research on perceiving, learning, and thinking eventually produced a wealth of data and facts describing these psychological *processes*, but the mind and its contents, the psychological *things*, remain products of reasoning, not research. In time, psychology's aether may join the luminiferous aether, in the historical archives of research, but for now the search for psychological things continues to cloud the modern understanding of psychology.

The mind has been reincarnated as the brain, and some psychologists still reason that psychological things such as images, ideas, and memories, must be stored there. Research on the brain has revealed neurophysiological structures and processes that are associated with psychological *processes*—but no psychological *things*.

Scientific advances often arise from unplanned discovery, rather than from planned research. In 1831, Charles Darwin embarked on a mission to collect biological data, holding no higher goal than to document the forms of life and habitats to be discovered on an ocean voyage; yet his discoveries serendipitously resulted in findings that led to an astonishing new account of the origin of life.

Even the so-called scientific method doesn't follow the rules of reason. Let's look at a simplified example of an experiment that will illustrate how researchers routinely accept conclusions based on fallacious reasoning:

> THEORY: Mass attracts mass.
> HYPOTHESIS: If two large masses are placed
>   near each other, they should pull
>   closer together.
> EXPERIMENT: Two large iron spheres are
>   suspended side-by-side from a high
>   ceiling beam.
> RESULTS: The spheres pull toward each
>   other, rather than hanging perfectly
>   vertical.
> CONCLUSION: The results support the theory.

The reasoning is: *If* the theory is true, *then* the spheres will pull toward each other (symbolically expressed: if A then B). We find the spheres pull toward each other as predicted (B is true), so we conclude that the theory (A) is true. But to conclude that the theory (A) is supported by the behavior of the spheres (B) is a logical fallacy known as *affirming the consequent*, which we recall from Chapter 4. Logically, we can only conclude from the research findings that the theory *may* be true; that is, the experimental results did not refute the theory. Yet the researcher will conclude that the data support the theory, and other researchers are likely to accept that conclusion. Even though their reasoning may be fallacious, scientific researchers are not troubled; they go right on making progress by documenting events and testing theories. (For further discussion of this and related issues, see Meehl, 1990.)

A Brief History of Empirica

While the use of Empirica's methods for establishing truth can be traced back thousands of years, a particularly fertile period came during the Golden Age of Greece. In the fifth century BCE, Thucydides wrote *History of the Peloponnesian War* and Herodotus wrote *Histories* to document Greece's victory in the Persian War. By modern standards these two writings lacked rigorous factual research, but for the time, both works set new standards for objectivity. As a result, Herodotus has been given the title Father of History and Thucydides is called the father of scientific history.

In China, details of celestial movements were recorded in the fourth century BCE, in the Era of Warring States, and during the Han Period. In the same century, Aristotle was researching and documenting many plant and animal types, and describing the functions of the human psyche, for which he could rightly be considered the founder of both biology and psychology. Callippus, a Greek mathematician working with Aristotle, applied mathematical calculations to recorded observation of celestial movements.

In the third century BCE, the Sicilian mathematician and inventor Archimedes of Syracuse advanced Empirica's truths with his research on physics. He is remembered primarily for Archimedes' Principle, which states that any floating object displaces its own weight in the fluid.

In the second century of the new millennium, Ptolemy, a Roman citizen living in Egypt, developed tables for predicting celestial movements. Ptolemy's geocentric (earth-centered) theory of the universe was, among astronomers, almost universally accepted until the sixteenth century. Also during the second century of the new millennium, the Roman physician and philosopher Galen of Pergamon described and analyzed human anatomy and physiology. Western medical students continued to study his teachings into the nineteenth century.

From the third through the fifth century, the authority of the Roman Church increased, leading to the Dark Ages. The truths of nature and history in the Western World fell under the authority of the Church, and the dissemination of scientific and historical truths that disagreed with authorized Christian beliefs were suppressed. For nearly a thousand years, the Church discouraged concern with the material world, and presented the purpose of life as preparation for the afterlife.

By the sixteenth century, the power of the Roman Church was declining, and, along with a renaissance in art and philosophy, the domain of Empirica reasserted itself. Interest in research on the structures and processes of the natural world grew. In 1543, nearing death, the Polish astronomer Nicolaus Copernicus received the first printing of his book, *De revolutionibus orbium coelestium* (*On the Revolutions of the Celestial Spheres*). This book, printed at the urgings of colleagues despite the author's apprehensions, presented conclusive evidence for a heliocentric (sun-centered) planetary system. The then-controversial theory presented the earth as a planet that spins while it orbits the sun.

The invention of the telescope in 1608 opened the door to rapid advances in astronomy. In 1610 Galileo Galilei, a prominent mathematician and scientist at the University of Padua, published *Sidereus Nuncius* (*Starry Messenger*), a book that presented telescopic observations of the moons of Jupiter, observations that were consistent with the Copernican theory of the solar system. Galileo's advocacy of the heliocentric theory put him at odds with official Church doctrine that placed the earth at the center of the universe. During the papacy of Urban VIII, Galileo was warned against continued advocacy of heliocentric theory, and in 1633 he was put on trial and found guilty of violating the Church's restraint. He was admonished, forced to recant heliocentric theory, and placed under house arrest.

But the Church could not stop the progress of astronomy. In Prague, Galileo's contemporary Johannes Kepler, a German astronomer, refined heliocentric theory using data collected by Danish nobleman Tycho Brahe and Tycho's sister Sophia. Kepler's analysis showed that the orbits of planets were not circular, as Copernicus had proposed sixty-six years earlier, but elliptical, and this accounted for some previously inexplicable movements of the planets.

The seventeenth century brought a full-scale scientific revolution, centered in England. Robert Boyle summarized the inverse relationship between the pressure and volume of gas, and proposed a new approach to chemistry based on elements. Robert Hooke discovered that life forms were made up of microscopic cells, and changed forever the course of biology. By documenting the mathematical relations of force to mass and motion, Isaac Newton produced a mathematical and mechanistic description of physical forces.

Empirica was maturing as an accepted path to truth and understanding, and from the beginning of the eighteenth century onward, the influence of empirical truth grew rapidly. By the second half of the nineteenth century, the sciences were evolving into separate academic disciplines. Astronomy, physics, chemistry, biology, and psychology were developing their own unique research laboratories, methods, and archives. The sciences were poised for an unprecedented era of discovery and progress.

The Promise and the Threat

In the twentieth century, expectations for scientific and technological progress were high, and unprecedented advances were occurring in communication, travel, medicine, engineering, agriculture, and education. While many people, especially the young, wanted faster progress, some older people longed for the simplicity of the past.

Now, in the twenty-first century, people are frightened by threats that scientific understanding and technology have made possible: global warming, drug-resistant microorganisms, nuclear accidents, international terrorism, loss of privacy, and others. But now we must again turn to

Empirica for the essential facts for dealing with these problems.

6

Four Sovereign Domains

THE FOUR DOMAINS of truth are metaphorical territories, but they have real and tangible institutions staffed by ordained elders with qualifications specific to their domain. The institutions include Rhetorica's capitals and courthouses, Mystica's churches and temples, Logica's colleges and universities, and Empirica's laboratories and museums. Elders who preside in these institutions must master the methods for testing truth *in their domain*. Judges master court rules, ministers master scriptures and dogmas, professors master logical reasoning, and scientists master methods of scientific research. The elders also enforce the tests of truth specific to their domains, defending them against all corrupting influences.

The ideal democracy can be defined as a government in which all four domains function freely. Legislators, judges, and editors are free to follow established rules of persuasion and debate as they reach decisions about what is just and true. Clerics and ideologues are free to follow and promote the truths of their faith. Professors are accorded academic freedom to teach students how to question and reason. And scientists and historians are allowed to follow wherever their data lead. In this ideal democracy, the only restrictions on the search for truth come in the form of laws designed to preserve the social order and protect individual rights and commercial interests. Even in such an ideal democracy, the sovereignty of each domain would still be threatened by other domains, as well as by cultural changes, and these threats would often distract elders from their search for truth.

When one domain gains enough power to influence law and social order, it can dominate the other domains. In the medieval period, Mystica gained sufficient authority to dominate the search for truth in the Western World. After centuries of oppression, protestant dissent gradually weakened the Roman Church's grip and contributed to the decline in Mystica's influence on Western thought. Rhetorica, Logica, and Empirica eventually regained their sovereignty and became competitive with Mystica. In today's modern democracies, the four domains generally enjoy mutual respect and cooperation, but inevitable disagreements between domains lead each to try to influence or dominate the others. Recent examples in the United States include displays of the Ten Commandments in courthouses, creation of new laws that define human zygotes and embryos as humans, the requirement that science textbooks identify evolution is only a theory, and the revisionist editing of historical facts to make them conform to a political bias.

As elders of all four domains vigorously defend their methods and truths, they must remain vigilant against foreign tests of truth that filter in from the other domains. Each domain must struggle to maintain the integrity of its tests of truth, its intellectual identity, and its influence on society.

Rhetorica's Sovereignty

The rules of formal debate guide the search for truth in Rhetorica, and these rules enjoy a special role in a democracy. Rules of persuasion and debate structure the search for truth in the legislative and judicial branches of democratic government. In legislative sessions, the rules of order are strict and those who master them gain considerable power in controlling the process. If the rules are violated, someone is likely to raise a "point of order" to bring the debate back in line with parliamentary rules. Similarly, in court proceedings, judges enforce forensic rules, and attorneys who master these rules gain an advantage in winning legal debates.

Laws have been fashioned to protect these institutions of government from influence by the tests of truth of Mystica,

Logica, or Empirica. Lawmakers and judges rigorously enforce their rules, and anyone who attempts to replace the search for truth through formal debate with a search for truth through divine revelation, methods of logic, or scientific research, may be ignored or ruled out of order.

Editorial rules are seldom strictly enforced, and in recent years they have been relaxed even further. At one time, editors tried to maintain editorial rules to minimize false assertions, but today, with a few exceptions, editors are more concerned with sponsors, sales, and survival, and less concerned about adequately vetting what they report. Sensational and controversial reports that were once limited to the tabloid press and talk radio are becoming commonplace in newspapers and network television news programs.

On June 7, 2011, *The New York Times* published a story on the internet under this headline: *Up to 30 Dismembered Bodies Found, Reuters Reports*. The location was a rural area near Houston and the dismembered bodies included children. The same story was also reported on other sites. The next day the newspaper released a correction stating that no bodies had been found.

This story represents an all-too-common problem with the news media: editors allow reports to go out without adequate review. In this case they identified their sources (Reuters), but that was not adequate. A day or two later readers learned that a psychic's tip had led to the report. A truth from Mystica had been presented as true in Rhetorica. This editorial process of sharing unvetted information, leaving readers to judge for themselves what is true, compromises the integrity of journalism in particular and the sovereignty of Rhetorica in general.

Mystica's Sovereignty

Democratic states allow a variety of faiths, but in theocracies the temples of unsanctioned faiths may be restricted or destroyed. For example, America's constitutional democracy grants religious freedom, but the theocratic Islamic Republic of Iran is controlled by Shiite Mullahs who suppress other religions and even other Islamic sects.

The methods of Rhetorica are often used to test articles of faith, thereby violating Mystica's integrity. In her 1999 book *Faith on Trial*, Pamela Binnings Ewen attempts to validate Christian beliefs by presenting forensic evidence allegedly bearing on the death and resurrection of Jesus. Since spiritual beliefs cannot be meaningfully refuted or confirmed by rhetorical debate, Ewen's mock trial was unnecessary and irrelevant. In the temples of Mystica, spiritual revelation and sacred texts, not the forensic debate of evidence, determines what is accepted as true.

Rhetorical arguments against a religion are just as pointless as those in favor of it. John Shelby Spong, the Episcopal Bishop of Newark, argued that modern understanding is incompatible with many Christian beliefs. Bishop Spong (1991 & 1999) described some traditional truths of Christian faith as outmoded in the post-Copernican, post-Newtonian, post-Darwinian, post-Freudian world. But Spong made the error of testing

Christian beliefs with rhetorical arguments, and thereby desecrated the temples of Mystica. Whether one agrees with him or not, he has been rightly criticized by Christian elders.

Because reason is often used to question faith rather than to confirm it, Mystica's temple elders generally reject the corrupting influence of reason. The early Christian Father Augustine preempted the intrusion of logic, saying, "If those who are called philosophers, and especially the Platonists, have aught that is true and in harmony with our faith, we are not only not to shrink from it, but to claim it for our own...." By selectively embracing assertions of Plato and his followers, Augustine and other Church Fathers took care not to test Christian truths with the methods of Logica.

In most temples of Islamic faith, logical analysis of sacred teachings was, and is, tolerated only within narrow limits. A thousand years have passed since the Muslim Mu'tazilah School of Theology promoted a more rational interpretation of the Quran. The Mu'tazilah School originated in Basra, Iraq, in the eighth century, and was opposed by the Ash'arite School made up of fundamentalists who saw the Quran as eternal and unalterable revelations from Allah that should never be viewed through the lens of reason. After centuries of relentless attack, the Mu'tazilah School faded away, although some Islamic sects retained much of its theology.

The famous Hindu guru, Swami Muktananda, founder of the Siddha Yoga movement, states in *Meditate* (1980) that logical reasoning is useless in the search for God. "Since that being is our innermost consciousness, it is necessary for us to turn within to have a direct experience of it." Muktananda was right—elders of Mystica should never try to discover or establish revealed truth with Logica's methods of reason.

Some evangelical Christians have corrupted their temple by introducing the methods of Empirica as tests of the truths of faith. In their book *In Search of Noah's Ark* (1976), David W. Balsiger and Charles E. Sellier, Jr., state: "Archeology not only authenticates Genesis, but hundreds of other Bible passages." Even if this claim were factual—and it is not—it would be irrelevant, since faith in biblical teachings and personal revelations requires no scientific authentication, actual or contrived. Beliefs rely on research findings no more than they do on rational proofs. Moreover, biblical teachings are not expressed in a way that opens them to refutation or authentication by archeological research.

In the temples of Mystica, beliefs are known to be true simply because they are revealed as true, and the act of believing in revelation constitutes a demonstration of faith. In defending Jesus' resurrection in the flesh, Tertullian of Carthage, a Father of Latin Christianity in the second and third centuries, asserted: "...*credibile est, quia ineptum est*...(it is certain, because it is impossible)." Tertullian's point is that the faithful must believe in the impossible, not because asserting the impossible is rhetorically persuasive (as Tertullian's apologists have argued), but because devout Christians search for truth in Mystica where miracles (things that may be factually impossible) are not only possible, but their occurrence is taken as verification of the existence of divine spiritual forces.

People who search for truth in Mystica must respect the sanctity of its temples, and must refrain from charades that attempt to test Mystica's truths with foreign methods. A clergy whose truths must pass the test of reason would be a faculty; a congregation whose truths are affirmed by forensic debate would be a jury; and a cleric whose truths are derived from and confirmed by research findings would be a scientist.

Logica's Sovereignty

Liberal arts colleges are the institutions of reason. Within their walls, scholars are free to apply the test of reason to all assertions of truth. For centuries, colleges have provided sanctuary to professors and scholars who serve as Logica's elders, allowing them to establish and enforce the rules of logic and to require their students to follow these rules in search of truth.

The primary threat to the sovereignty of Logica's institutions comes in an unexpected form: Governmental agencies hold some of the purse strings for public colleges, and religious orders provide funding for church-affiliated schools. In both cases, financial support may come with contingencies limiting what can or should be taught, or what faculty members and students are allowed to do or say. In order to shield themselves from such constraints, Logica's elders promote the concept of academic freedom, and award tenure to senior faculty members.

To counter what they perceive as liberal social rhetoric in educational institutions, politically conservative commentators often argue that campuses need to provide a balanced debate between the political right and left. In a newspaper column published in June 2004, conservative columnist John Leo spoke for many when he said: "Arguing is crucial to education." Of course it is dialectical argument, not a balance of partisan rhetoric, which must be protected in the institutions of Logica. Leo's approach would remake colleges into forums for partisan rhetoric, and have them busily hosting political debates.

Rhetorical attacks on Logica's integrity can be traced back thousands of years. During the Golden Age of Greece, sophists introduced Rhetorica's methods of debate into Logica, and became subversives in the brotherhood of scholars, using rhetorical arguments to persuade students to distrust the truths of Logica. According to the sophists, when logical conclusions fly in the face of common sense, it is logic, not common sense, which we should distrust.

Philosophers such as Descartes, Spinoza, Leibniz, and Locke, and many others who served as elders of Logica, used the methods of logic in an attempt to prove the existence of God. What these philosophers actually proved, if anything, was that some of the most renowned philosophers were willing to desecrate Logica with rational arguments intended to defend religious beliefs. Since logic cannot serve as an acceptable test for truths of faith, any rational proof of God's existence is not only pointless, it is also a distraction from Logica's pursuit of reasoned truth.

Sometimes empirical research findings are innocently cited as validation of the truths of Logica. For example, a creative engineering student may test mathematical equations or geometric theorems with empirical methods. While such tests may be reassuring to students, they do not provide proof of the validity of equations or theorems. Measurement of the sides of any number of right triangles may or may not support the Pythagorean theorem, but the data obtained can neither prove nor disprove the theorem. Intrusions of empirical research methods into Logica do little harm, so long as they are not presented as a means to prove the truths of Logica.

In *The Grand Design* (2010), Stephen Hawking and Leonard Mlodinow say that "...philosophy is dead," because it has not "kept up with modern developments in science...." If it is true that philosophers have not kept up with contemporary science, it is equally true that they did not necessarily need to do so. They need only keep abreast of advances in the methods and truths of logical reasoning. As long as that distinction is clear, the elders of Logica will not be confused with or by the elders of Empirica.

Empirica's Sovereignty

Research laboratories, science libraries, museums, and archival libraries are the institutions of Empirica, and scientists and historians serve as the domain's elders. Empirica's institutions may be modest workrooms or huge complexes bristling with technology, but regardless of the size, complexity, and purpose of laboratories, individuals who apply for admission are expected to master and rigorously abide by the rules and ethics of empirical research.

While many research laboratories and science libraries are private, most are affiliated with large universities, and just as academic freedom is critical to the integrity of Logica, research freedom is essential to the integrity of Empirica. Funding for research projects may come from a university, governmental agency, private foundation, advocacy group, or commercial organization. When advocacy or commercial organizations fund research, a potential conflict of interest exists between the desire to retain grant funding and the necessity of insuring that research findings are not biased in favor of the goals of the funding organization.

Perhaps the greatest threat to the sovereignty of Empirica comes from journalists. Science reporters are eager to announce new breakthroughs and their reports of scientific advances often outstrip the actual progress. Since few journalists fully understand research design and the analysis of data, it is no surprise that they often publish misleading reports of research projects and findings. Terms such as "correlation coefficient," "statistical significance," and, "percent of accountable variance" entail certain assumptions, and have precise and complex meanings that may elude journalists, leading to inaccurate reports on the purpose, design, and findings of research. Moreover, journalists sometimes fail to convey the distinction between advances in scientific understanding and advances in technology. Scientific research typically requires complex technology, and new technologies are usually made possible by scientific knowledge, but an advance in one should not be presumed to be an advance in the other. There is a clear divide between the methods and goals of engineering and the methods and goals of physical science.

The terminology of other domains sometimes wreaks havoc in Empirica. Several years ago, a major television network news anchor introduced a research report on the risk/benefit ratio from frequent mammography screening in certain age groups. The anchor cut to a fellow reporter for the "cold, hard facts," and then a medical expert was asked for an "opinion," and finally a second medical expert was asked if she still had "faith" in mammography screening for breast cancer. In that one brief episode, the terminology for the truths of the various domains was hopelessly mangled, and viewers were left with little or no understanding of what researchers had actually found. This may seem like an extreme example of journalistic confusion, but it is distressingly common.

Research findings are seldom simple or definitive, and in interviews, researchers may offer technical equivocations that bore most viewers and readers. After a plane crash, before the smoke has cleared, reporters look for the cause, growing more impatient each time accident investigators tell them that definitive answers are weeks or months away. Such research is too technical, too equivocal, and too slow to be newsworthy, leaving reporters to turn to "experts" willing to give them instant opinions and analyses, before the research work has even begun. But if they happen to consult true experts, they will encounter more equivocation.

For centuries, incursions of religious beliefs into Empirica have threatened the sovereignty of its institutions, and those threats continue to the present day. Many Christians believe that the life and soul of a person is created at conception. Because President George W. Bush held this view, he saw abortion as the killing of a human being, and banned the funding of research that required embryonic stem cells obtained from aborted four to five day old blastocysts or young embryos. The ban dashed high hopes held by many medical researchers for finding cures for serious and debilitating maladies. President Bush's successor, President Barack Obama, removed this restriction on research.

It is not uncommon for politicians to attempt to correct science and history by using their religious and ideological beliefs to differentiate "good" science from "bad" science. As noted earlier, three of eight candidates seeking the Republican nomination for president in 2007 admitted that they did not "believe" in evolution. A president guided by biblical teachings of creation could have major effects on the availability of funding for biological research and the teaching of biology. A science that is required to conform its theories and facts to biblical teachings or political ideologies would, however, be a science no more.

In an attempt to gain credibility, some faith-based belief systems—astrology, phrenology, and parapsychology, for example—have claimed to be sciences. In 1925 Joseph B. Rhine received his Ph.D. in botany from the University of Chicago, and in 1935 he established a laboratory at Duke University, specifically designed for researching paranormal phenomena. Rhine reported that his research provided evidence for extrasensory perception (ESP), but in fact he never subjected ESP to the rigorous tests of traditional research. A few subjects in his research projects typically guessed much better than chance, and as a result were identified as possibly having ESP. But a small percentage of subjects would always be expected to guess well above average by chance (balanced by approximately the same percentage who would guess with accuracy far below chance). Because of Rhine's non-standard research techniques, plus reported instances of questionable research control in his laboratory, most experimental psychologists saw little credibility in his work, and after Rhine retired in 1965, Duke closed its parapsychology laboratory. Many people still consider parapsychology to be a science, but it emerged from, and is sustained by, belief in the paranormal, not by research findings.

Faith-based truths are often held with such certainty that believers expect scientific research to confirm their beliefs. Moreover, believers often assume that the wisdom of personal revelation leads them to the truth about reality more quickly and more accurately than science can.

Let us look again at *Meditate*, where Swami Muktananda provides an example of belief claiming precedence over science. He argues that today's scientists are coming to understand that "the basis of the universe is energy." In doing so, they discover "what the ancient sages of India have known for millennia": that consciousness "...forms the ground, or canvas, on which the material universe is drawn." In fact, he says: "...the entire world is the play of this energy... [which] becomes all the forms and shapes we see around us."

Muktananda's views have no relevance to Empirica. Just as faith cannot profit from verification based in empirical fact, the pursuit of facts cannot profit from the transcendent wisdom of faith, no matter how ancient or widespread. Muktananda misses the meaning of the word *energy* as conceived by the physicists whom he would instruct, and conversely, few physicists would claim to understand Muktananda's concept of *energy*. Scientists who want to understand Muktananda must abandon the methods of Empirica, at least temporarily, to pursue the revealed truths of Mystica.

Fritjof Capra, founder and director of the Center for Ecoliteracy in Berkeley, California, is among those physicists who have taken the journey into mysticism. In the *Tao of Physics* (1991), he argues that: "there is an essential harmony between the spirit of Eastern Wisdom and Western science." Capra presumes that real truths are universal, transcending all tests, and that revelations of Daoism must therefore be in "essential harmony" with facts of science. Even though Capra's writings fascinate readers looking for a way to merge religious faith with scientific understanding, the elders of Empirica must firmly reject any use of the methods of faith in establishing the facts of nature.

Just as philosophers draw freely on facts established in science and history, researchers draw freely from the truths of mathematics and logic; even so, research findings, not logical tests, must always arbitrate the truths of Empirica. Many scientific theories are quite reasonable, but even so, they may not be factual. For example, Ptolemy's geocentric theory of the universe was reasonable but not factual. And conversely, scientific facts need not be reasonable, and may not even be understandable. The Nobel Laureate Richard Feynman said, in 1965: "I think I can safely say that nobody understands Quantum Mechanics." Whether it is rationally understandable or not, quantum theory has passed Empirica's tests of research and is generally accepted as factually true.

An Uneasy Détente

The four domains of truth have been in conflict since their inception. Contradictions between domains can never be resolved, but they can be identified and tolerated—if their elders and advocates respect the sovereignty of the institutions of the other domain. When proponents of one domain seek to instruct or attack another, they do nothing to improve the search for truth in either domain.

Elders must assume the right and obligation to defend and enforce the rules of their domain. Truth-seekers entering the institutions of any domain must understand and accept the applicable rules. In judicial proceedings, participants must abide by the court's rules and authority; those who do not may be ejected or charged with contempt. In religious settings and ceremonies, truth-seekers who criticize the revelations of the prophets, or the beliefs of the sect, quickly find that they are not welcome in its temples. Freshmen who chafe under the strictures of formal logic will find many college classrooms uncomfortable, and those who reject research findings need not apply for admission to the laboratories of Empirica.

Domain elders borrow and use the truths and methods of other domains for practical purposes. For example, scientists tend to follow the rules of reason in developing theories, formulating research methods, and analyzing experimental findings, but these logical methods establish no empirical facts. Indeed, scientists who would use borrowed methods to test and establish truth violate the sovereignty of their own domain; and scientists who expect empirical facts to be discovered through reasoning will find that other scientists recognize their assertions as untested hypotheses, not as facts.

Borrowed truths may be cast aside if they prove inconvenient. For example, attorneys selectively use the truths of religion, reason, and science in their arguments; but only when these borrowed truths support their side in the debate. Similarly, theologians may accept laws and conventional wisdom, logical deductions, and research findings, provided these borrowed truths do not conflict with the articles of their faith. Logicians question all methods and assertions of truth, but they also may stipulate the truths of any domain for the sake of dialectical discussion. And scientists follow reasoned inferences right up to the point where reasoned conclusions conflict with research data.

In the Dark Ages, Mystica dominated the search for truth; in the Age of Reason, Logica grew to contest Mystica's dominance; and in the twentieth century, Empirica progressed so quickly that it overshadowed the progress of other domains. In recent years, the balance of power has shifted again, this time toward Rhetorica. With the rise of electronic media, persuasion and debate have become the primary methods for testing the truth of public assertions. Celebrities, experts, commentators, politicians, attorneys, and journalists of every stripe crowd the public forums, promoting their opinions. People increasingly look to news commentators and internet bloggers, and even social media commentators to provide the truth.

Today, Rhetorica's elders—politicians, attorneys, and journalists—will debate which religious practices are acceptable and which are not, what should be taught in colleges and what should not, and what is "good" science and what is "bad." Rhetorica reigns supreme in this Information Age, and elders of the other domains struggle to protect the sovereignty of their institutions, hoping to avoid a new Dark Age ruled by Rhetorica. It is the task of educators to learn, preserve, and teach the formal methods of all four domains, and to provide students with the skills to manage the flood of unvetted information now available to them at the touch of a button or screen.

7

Handling Truth

UNDERSTANDING, LIKE THE lens in a telescope, is transparent. We do not see our understanding, we see the world through our understanding. From the time we are born, our lens of understanding grows clearer and stronger, gradually bringing distant worlds into sharper focus.

Over the early years of life, understanding grows rapidly, becoming at once more complex and more effortless. Children learn about the world as they experience it, and they ask who, what, when, where, how, and why, rapidly learning what others know.

As children accumulate bits and pieces of understanding, they fit them together, much like a mental jigsaw puzzle. Many newly acquired pieces of the puzzle fall readily into place, while others do not fit at all and are rejected, or are used to start new isolated sections of the puzzle. The puzzle grows rapidly, but occasionally it fragments into separate and incompatible sections, compartmentalizing understanding and sending us on a lifelong struggle to unite isolated parts of our understanding. Occasionally, new and fascinating truths allow us to restructure and unite major parts, but all too often odd pieces are forced into places where they do not fit.

For those who master their puzzle—that is, their composite of understanding—four large but incompatible sections may finally emerge, corresponding to the four domains of truth. Throughout our lives, we continue to search for missing pieces for our puzzles, but by middle age most of us have become resistant to new ideas, taking truth like good wine, selectively and in moderation. Truth hardens into a well-worn repertoire, and the search for truth all but ends for many. For a lucky few, new ideas remain irresistible, and the discovery of new truths is still intoxicating.

Even if we still search for truth, most new assertions we encounter do not receive consideration for incorporation into our puzzle. Each new assertion must pass through a three-step screening process. When an assertion passes through all three filters, we then try to fit it into our puzzle.

Screening Truths

The first filter screens out sources of information that lack credibility, such as those considered foolish, misguided, biased, or evil. The second filter eliminates truths that fall outside the bounds of personal interest, and the third filter rejects assertions that challenge personal comprehension. Only a small fraction of the assertions we encounter pass through all three filters.

Credible Sources

We select among the available sources of truth, choosing the people we listen to, the texts we read, the programs we watch, and the places we go. We tend to rule out sources that appear dishonest, that disagree with our political or religious views, that bear unacceptable accents or grammar, or that are strange or foreign. We reject almost instantly assertions from sources that we find unacceptable, greatly reducing the number of assertions that go on to the second filter. Of course, some of these rejected assertions may still slip through to the second filter, if they happen to be recalled after their source is forgotten.

Interesting Issues

Our interests are framed by experience, culture, and personal needs. Childhood interests fade, to be replaced by adolescent and then adult interests. Just as we tire of a repetitive diet, we can satisfy an intellectual interest and move on to something new. Topics that were once fascinating become boring, and we may find ourselves in a continuous search for new interests. Whatever our interests of the moment, they dominate what we are willing to listen to and learn about. This second screening step usually takes only a few seconds, and only those few assertions that pass through can reach the third and final screening.

Understandable Truth

The third filter is based on personal knowledge and understanding, plus our willingness to work at the task of learning something new. If we have difficulty understanding an assertion, we tend to ignore it. For example, technicalities of law, theology, philosophy, science, technology, art, and music are typically ignored by most of us, unless we have special training in those fields. But we occasionally face circumstances that compel us to pursue difficult subjects. As students we try to understand the proofs in mathematics courses (at least long enough to pass the exams). When ill, we struggle to understand the relationship between disease and treatment. As citizens summoned to court, we try to learn the intricacies of the justice system. But for the most part, we leave these more complicated areas of understanding to the experts.

Which Domain?

When an assertion passes the screening process, we test it by determining if it will fit into one of the sections of our puzzle of truth. But which one? This is the most important question in the personal search for truth. The placement we select determines whether the new assertion fits and is accepted as true, or does not fit and is rejected as false. If we have organized the major parts of our puzzle in accordance with the four domains of truth, we can more easily see where the new assertion should fit. If, however, an assertion is placed with truths of an inappropriate domain or subjected to an inappropriate test, it will probably be rejected—or if not rejected, forced into a place where it does not fit.

Consider this simple statement of fact: *Human beings evolved from earlier primates.* The truth of the statement can be evaluated for inclusion in any one of the four domains, but the domain selected determines whether the statement is accepted or rejected. If it is assigned to Mystica, we may reject it by saying, "The scriptures do not agree with the 'theory' of evolution."

To create a similar mismatch between assertion and domain, consider this scriptural assertion: *Adam and Eve were the first human beings.* Were it assigned to Empirica, we would reject it with the observation, "Research shows evolutionary change rather than a single point of human appearance."

For many assertions of truth, the domain of origin is evident:

> Democracy is the best form of government.
>   —RHETORICA
> There will be an accounting for our sins in the
>   afterlife. —MYSTICA
> If a coin lands on heads ten times in succession,
>   the probability it will land on heads on
>   the eleventh toss is 50-50. —LOGICA

> High blood pressure increases the probability of
> a heart attack. —EMPIRICA

Each of these assertions is likely to be judged by its fit with the truths of the domain in which it obviously originated.

Some assertions seem to belong to no particular domain. Consider this statement: *There is intelligent life in outer space.* Is this asserted as a debatable proposition, an unwavering belief, a logical inference, or a researched fact? A probe into the domain of origin is necessary before the truth of the statement can be fairly assessed. To elicit clues about the origin of an assertion, we may ask the person making the statement: How do you know? If the statement is an opinion, it will be defended with persuasive arguments, perhaps testimonials from people who claim to have seen UFOs. If the statement is offered as an article of faith, its promoter may supply references to supportive scripture or prophesy. If the statement is a logical proposition, the assumptions and lines of logical reasoning or mathematical probabilities are likely to emerge, and if it is asserted as an empirical fact, there will likely be a reference to published research in a reputable journal of science. Once we are sure of the domain of origin, we can see how well the statement fits with other truths of that domain, and then appropriately accept or reject it.

Irreconcilable Disagreement

Disagreements between domains cannot be resolved, they can only be accepted. In describing Aristotle's views on *muthos* (Mystica) and *logos* (Logica), Charles Freeman, in *The Closing of the Western Mind* (2004), states that Aristotle emphasized the lack of conflict between the two domains: "Each has its value in its own context and neither threatens the other." Aristotle recognized that the truths of faith need not be reconciled with truths of logic, because faith and logic lead to different kinds of truth.

Nothing so frustrates the search for truth as attempting to bring all views to the table, to take a multi-disciplinary approach and seek common ground among domains. There can be no common ground among the four domains. A disagreement cannot be resolved when one person is debating, another person is proselytizing, a third person is demanding logical proofs, and a fourth accepts only replicated research findings. Communication immediately breaks down as each of the four discussants defines the terms of the statement in ways that are unacceptable to the other three. That is not to say that truths cannot be borrowed from other domains, but when truths of two domains disagree, the dispute can be resolved only by ignoring or rejecting the truths from the foreign domain.

Reconcilable Disagreement

Assume that a friend asserts, "Abortion is murder." The statement may quickly pass all three screening filters by: 1) originating from an acceptable source, 2) having sufficient interest, and 3) being comprehensible. But is the statement an opinion the speaker is advocating? Is it the result of a religious belief? Is it a reasoned inference logically drawn from sound premises? Is it a reference to a documented historical fact of law? In other words, in which domain did the assertion originate?

If we should disagree with our friend's assertion, what would be the nature of the disagreement? Is it just a difference of opinion, or does the disagreement arise because we are operating in two different domains? Once we agree on the applicable domain—and it may be any one of the four—the points of disagreement become clear, and resolution of our disagreement may be possible. If we cannot agree on a single domain, then no resolution is possible. We must agree to disagree.

Disagreement within Rhetorica

Disagreement is always welcomed within the borders of Rhetorica. Disagreements may be planned and arranged even before there is an assertion to dispute. Candidates from opposing political parties arrange debates, knowing they will find many points of disagreement to fill the time allotted for the scheduled debate. In court debates, the prosecuting attorney and defense counsel prepare as a matter of course to disagree with each other. Formal debates within Rhetorica may be judged and a winner declared, resolving the disagreement—at least to the satisfaction of those who made the judgment and, of course, the winning side.

Disagreement within Mystica

Within Mystica's borders, disputes occur only when there are conflicting beliefs. A Catholic and a Muslim may disagree vehemently about the trinity, and either side may condemn the beliefs of the other as heresy. With such stark and absolute positions, neither side can prevail so debate is pointless. Only when both parties respectfully and peacefully agree to disagree can the outcomes be acceptable to both believers.

As theologians of the same faith conduct an exegesis of their holy texts, it is possible to resolve disagreements in interpretation. Consider the lasting effects of the Nicene Creed adopted in the year 325 at the First Council of Nicaea. Through it, an official Christian truth was established, that Jesus Christ, the Son of God, is of one substance with the Father—an idea that remains incomprehensible to many outside the Christian faith, but within the Christian faith the dispute was and is settled.

Disagreement within Logica

Within Logica, disagreement focuses on a proposition, such as: A person's brain cannot logically be the controller of the person. To which a doubter might ask, "Why do you think so? What is your reasoning?" A dialectical discussion could ensue in which the truth of the proposition would be analyzed. If a logical proof (or disproof) of the proposition emerges, the disagreement is thereby resolved.

Disagreement within Empirica

Factual disagreement requires examination of the research that gave rise to an asserted fact. Researchers who report conflicting findings may disagree vigorously, but usually their disagreements revolve around questions of research design or methods of data analysis. It is quite acceptable for scientists to argue with each other, but not with the data. In time, the force of new data tends to resolve all disputes in Empirica—but invariably it also raises new questions. There will always be new questions, new theories, and new data. There will be no final scientific truth, just the facts as scientists know them at any given point in time. This is not to say the facts we know today are unreliable or likely to fail us. Over the twentieth century, basic scientific understanding became extraordinarily reliable.

Lies and Deceit

Beyond confusion resulting from different ways of testing truth, and honest disagreements arising within each domain, there remains the issue of deception and mendacity. When we lie, we misrepresent what we know. Of course, what we know generally comes from personal experience and has not passed any test of truth, so lying about what we know is of little consequence in the greater search for truth. But public misrepresentations of the outcome of formal tests in any domain can harm that domain. Each domain attempts to protect itself from this type of harm by stating and enforcing the ethical standards and practices of the domain.

Deceit in Rhetorica

Misrepresentation of truth in Rhetorica dismays no one. In this contentious domain, we expect bias and conflict of interest to compromise honesty, and they usually do. Bias is never more obvious than in the adversarial roles taken by prosecutors and defense attorneys. Jurors must understand the bias inherent in the adversarial system, and realize that neither side can be trusted to tell all it knows. Both sides seek to sway, not to enlighten, the jury.

It is no accident that many politicians start out as lawyers. The fine art of partisan rhetoric that serves so well in the courtroom also provides a useful foundation for swaying the electorate. While canvassing for votes, many political candidates, whether formally trained as lawyers or not, begin to blur the lines of veracity with vague promises and sweeping pronouncements, waxing eloquent about the wisdom of their party and the foolishness of their opponent's party. They may even stoop to unsubstantiated accusations about their opponent's conduct or motives, and in the Information Age, even adolescent name-calling has become an acceptable method for swaying the electorate—at least in America.

People tend to vote for the candidate who says things they want to hear, and winning candidates usually tailor their public statements to maximize their appeal and garner votes. Many otherwise-honest politicians have felt the lure of playing to the biases and fears of their constituents, deceiving them in minor ways in order to obtain their support. Deceit and demagoguery are often rewarded in Rhetorica, and our only defense against them is a free press and an educated public. A press that routinely publicizes and critiques the words and actions of political leaders allows the governed some opportunity to be informed rather than deceived and deluded.

A free press is essential to democracy. It would be foolish to accept, into any debate of truth, those press reports that originate from theocracies or dictatorships. Just as journalists in Nazi Germany or the Soviet Union tended to report the party line, journalists in some modern theocracies, dictatorships, and kingdoms make their reports of events agreeable to clerical leaders, dictators, and powerful monarchs.

Perhaps the most corrosive deceit in Rhetorica is to pretend to be debating while actually proselytizing for what we believe. When someone inquires about your views on religious or political issues, that person rarely wishes to enter into an authentic debate and, more likely, wants to proselytize. This form of deceit leaves many open-minded people reluctant to discuss their beliefs. Similarly, many politicians have become so dedicated to their political ideologies or lust for power that they can no longer engage in honest debate about political issues.

Deceit in Mystica

When our stated beliefs are belied by our conduct, the term *lie* is inappropriate. Such inconsistency is properly called *hypocrisy*. While it is tolerated in free societies, hypocrisy can be a more serious matter in theocratic states, where the inquisitors have power to persecute the unfaithful, and may deal harshly with hypocrites. After the Roman Church gained the power to enforce its truths in Europe, the fires of hell were felt by heretics who were burned at the stake. Ironically, the Church continued to deceive the faithful by selling indulgences—free passes to commit sins—and sacred relics, such as bits of cloth purported to be from a garment Jesus wore.

In much of the Muslim world, citizens live under the authority of Islamic law, and in countries where radical versions of Islam are practiced, individuals who convert to another faith may be sentenced to death. Fear can be a great motivator, so the prospect of execution could produce feigned devotion to faith, in which case disbelievers who are found out will be judged harshly for their hypocritical claims of faith.

Many constitutional democracies have long defended freedom of religion and struggled to maintain separation of church and state. Yet American politicians often publicize their church affiliation and boast about their strong belief in God, implying that their administration would support legislation consistent with Christian traditions. Whether their faith is real or a hypocritical expedient, their intent is clear: they are trying to convince Christian believers to vote for them.

In the last half of the twentieth century, American televangelists replaced tent revivalists in bringing Christian salvation to the masses. The motives and hypocrisy of many of these evangelists are too obvious to belabor, as they beg from the poor to maintain their own wealth, while promoting a faith that denounces the pursuit of earthly materialism. Hucksters and confidence men, operating under the veil of faith, have worked the airways and the internet with considerable success, but a few have stepped over the line and suffered the legal consequences. Jim Bakker, founder of The PTL (Praise The Lord) Club, rose to prominence in the 1980s, before being sent to prison for defrauding his followers.

Deceit in Logica

Reason is resistant to deception. Logica conducts its business out in the open and by clear rules. The scholar whose reasoning produces invalid inferences is treated as inept rather than deceitful, and in Logica ineptitude is held in particularly low regard. As David Hume said in 1739 in *A Treatise of Human Nature*: "Generally speaking, the errors in religion are dangerous; those in philosophy only ridiculous." If, however, someone intentionally breaches the rules of logic in order to deceive, that person may be exiled from the halls of Logica.

Deceitful reasoning in Logica is rare, but deceptive reasoning often occurs when there is external pressure or motivation. For example, the rules of reasoning provide the basis for the practice of accounting, and an accountant may be pressured to show profit where none exists. It is the auditor's job to force accountants to follow established rules of accounting, and if laws are violated an accountant can be prosecuted.

Deceit in Empirica

While Logica is resistant to deception, Empirica is extremely vulnerable. Each researcher relies on all other researchers to be conscientiously honest and self-critical. For that reason, the first principle taught to students of science or history is this: *Lying about a research finding is unconscionable and unpardonable.*

The presumption of truthfulness, and the trust engendered by that presumption, make lying all the more damaging. Science and history have their infamous liars, and both fields struggle to expel any researcher who fails the test of scrupulous honesty. In 1912 someone cleverly modified an ape jaw to fit a modern human skull, and represented the results as a find from an archeological site in East Sussex, England. This legendary Piltdown Man hoax created decades of confusion about human evolution. In 1953 the forgery was finally exposed though carbon dating, but the identity of the perpetrator and the motive for the hoax remain a mystery. It is noteworthy that it was new archeological research findings that led to rejection of Piltdown Man even before it was shown to be a fraud.

Although scientific deception is rare, Empirica has always been plagued with minor lying by marginal players. Occasionally, unethical researchers invent or distort findings to make them appear more interesting to colleagues, employers, or funding agencies. It would be naïve to think that all researchers resist the very real professional, social, and economic pressures to fudge their data. For this and other reasons, important factual findings must be replicated in other laboratories, and by different researchers with different motives, before those findings are fully accepted. All the cases of deceit notwithstanding, it is fair to say that the vast majority of people involved in *basic* scientific research maintain exemplary standards of honesty.

Deceiving Ourselves

We've all heard someone say, "You can't handle the truth." The implication is that some truths are really too threatening to be accepted. A child may ask, "Will I die some day?" The answer to this question is hard for the parents and child to handle, and might still be unnerving long after the child has become an adult. Most of us, regardless of age, face the prospect of death with some degree of denial. We may cloak the troubling finality of death with euphemisms such as "passing away" or "departing this life." In America it has become popular to say "If something happens to me" instead of saying "When I die."

We find euphemisms for many uncomfortable realities, and may be duped by our own euphemisms. Prisoners are locked in "correctional facilities." Enemies are "neutralized." Civilians killed in war are "collateral damage." Even atrocities can be cloaked in euphemisms. "Ethnic cleansing" has been used as a sanitary label for genocide, but the victims are dead, not cleaner.

Language can illuminate the truth or blind us to it. We can clearly and honestly express truth as we know it, or we can choose flowery words that protect us from the harsh realities, but words matter, and the road to liar's hell is paved with euphemisms.

Our belief systems may be designed to protect us from unpleasant realities. For example, many religions present death as a transition to a glorious afterlife, but that motivates only a few of the faithful to become martyrs. As the old saying goes, "Everybody wants to go to heaven, but nobody is in a hurry to get there." To "keep on the bright side," we may attempt to deceive ourselves about the nature of death, but we are unlikely to succeed completely.

Wandering among the Domains

There are times when each domain beckons. Politicians attempt to persuade us that their assertions are true and offer a better tomorrow, but only if we agree to follow and advance their political cause. Evangelists and gurus promise a blessed life and afterlife, if we follow their teaching and believe in *The Truth*. Scholars offer students a way to find truth, improve their understanding, and thereby enrich their intellectual lives, but only if the students stay in school and continue learning. Scientists may say little but their truths shout: "Here is the way the world works! Don't you want to know?"

We must learn to distinguish among the four domains, and then decide which one or ones we trust in our personal search for truth. The communications industry will not help us in forming our decision. It blends the voices of the four domains into a stew of "information" spiced with misunderstandings and mendacity. As we struggle to sort through this daily stream of misinformation, we must always remember to identify the domain of origin for each assertion, and to use the appropriate terminology.

The terms *opinion, belief, inference,* and *fact* are so carelessly and inaccurately applied that the real distinctions among them are often lost. We hear the expressions *in my opinion... I believe... it is reasonable to infer... in fact...* used more or less interchangeably, with no regard for the fact that the distinctions among these words are used to differentiate the truths of the four domains. The only way we can transcend this flood of information and recognize the deception is to learn to recognize the four types of truth and to apply that understanding conscientiously, in all situations.

8

The Truth-Seekers

JUST AS WE seldom reflect on our personal means of understanding, we are generally unaware of how our understanding has shaped our search for truth. Consider your own personal search: How did your unique life experiences lead to the paths you took in search of truth? Did some important event transform your search? Did you come to reject or avoid any domain? Did you develop a special respect for the elders of any domain?

To understand where your experiences have led you, begin by identifying the types of truths you trust. Do you place special trust in the debated truths of Rhetorica, the revealed truths of Mystica, the reasoned truths of Logica, or the factual truths of Empirica? The trust you place in the methods of each domain distinguishes your personal search for truth and determines which types of assertions you are likely to accept and which you are likely to reject.

Domains and Personalities

While we all have a personal history that guides us along our special paths to truth, we have each traveled in all four domains. We were drawn to the rules of Rhetorica when discussing politics, to truths of Mystica when making assertions about the unknowable, to Logica's methods when trying to solve critical problems, and to Empirica's facts when the topic was nature or history.

We each travel in the same four domains, but chance factors, opportunity, and personal biases put each of us on a unique path to truth. Some people tend to stay within one preferred domain, often Rhetorica, while others make themselves at home in each domain, but many of us are distinguished by our reluctance or refusal to enter the institutions of a particular domain.

By the way we select and reject domains, we narrow our search for truth and develop kinships with others who have made similar choices. We tend to respect and trust people who share the paths we take in searching for truth.

Our Personal Paths to Truth

To better understand the path you have chosen, analyze your level of trust in the truths of the four domains.

1. *My opinions*
    a. *Strongly trust*
    b. *Mildly trust*
    c. *Mildly distrust*
    d. *Strongly distrust*

2. *My beliefs*
    a. *Strongly trust*
    b. *Mildly trust*
    c. *Mildly distrust*
    d. *Strongly distrust*

3. *Logical proofs*
    a. *Strongly trust*
    b. *Mildly trust*
    c. *Mildly distrust*
    d. *Strongly distrust*

4. *Scientific research findings*
    a. *Strongly trust*
    b. *Mildly trust*
    c. *Mildly distrust*
    d. *Strongly distrust*

These self-assessment questions will help you position yourself in the following matrix of personality types based on domain preferences.

Domain Purists vs. the Critics

The most extreme approach one can take in the search for truth is to trust exclusively in one domain. Domain *purists* see their chosen domain as the only one that can be fully trusted. Purists are not necessarily masters or elders of their chosen domain, but they usually achieve a high level of understanding of its methods and truths, while remaining relatively unconcerned with, and perhaps uninformed about, the methods and truths of the other three domains. Although purists cannot avoid some degree of contact with the other three domains, they tend to ignore them.

Just as purists defend the truths of only one domain, *critics* single out one domain for persistent attack. The following table lists eight personality types, representing the two extremes, purists and critics, for each domain.

	PURISTS	**CRITICS**
Rhetorica	*Persuaders*	*Cynics*
Mystica	*Believers*	*Skeptics*
Logica	*Rationalists*	*Sophists*
Empirica	*Realists*	*Idealists*

Rhetorica: Persuaders vs. Cynics

Persuaders are down-to-earth people who may admit they are not experts in the truths of Mystica, Logica, or Empirica. They collect information on a wide array of topics, and they hold firm opinions, but are always willing to listen to the arguments of others. To persuaders, truth is never more certain than when people agree. They live in Rhetorica, but they will discuss and debate truths from any domain. When they visit institutions of other domains—churches, colleges, or research laboratories—persuaders may show interest and ask relevant questions, but they assume that the answers they receive (from clerics, scholars, or researchers) are, like the truths of Rhetorica, just judgments and opinions.

Persuaders are naturally attracted to professions in politics, law, and communications; but no matter which profession they choose, they continue to collect information, always willing to learn the opinions of others and to defend their own opinions. Examples of successful persuaders of our time include Presidents Ronald Reagan and Bill Clinton.

Critics, who poke fun at persuaders and the truths born in Rhetorica, are labeled *cynics*. Ambrose Bierce, one of the most unrepentant cynics of the nineteenth century, was a newspaper columnist, fiction writer, and author of *The Devil's Dictionary*—a collection of witty definitions that spoof all types of persuaders while exalting cynics:

> POLITICS: A strife of interests masquerading as a contest of principles. The conduct of public affairs for private advantage.

> LAWYER: One skilled in circumvention of the law.

> REPORTER: A writer who guesses his way to truth and dispels it with a tempest of words.

CYNIC: A blackguard whose faulty vision
sees things as they are, not as they
ought to be.

Because we tend to see finely honed rhetoric as a means
to obscure rather than to reveal the truth, many of us are
amused by such biting cynicism. We instinctively distrust
the eloquently defended assertions of politicians, lawyers,
and journalists. The humorous gibes of clever cynics of the
past, such as Voltaire, Jonathan Swift, Mark Twain, Oscar
Wilde, and H. L. Mencken, are still appreciated and
considered relevant by modern cynics.

Mystica: Believers vs. Skeptics

Believers search for the ultimate and final truths of
revelation and enlightenment, and are willing to accept the
truths of Rhetorica, Logica, and Empirica only when they do
not conflict with the revealed truths of their faith. While
believers seldom hold the methods and truths of science in
high regard, they are not reluctant to adopt the latest
technologies in order to proselytize more efficiently.
Proselytizers adapted their message to the new medium of
radio in the 1930s, to television in the 1960s, and more
recently to the internet.

Believers often retreat to remote or private places to
meditate and to study their sources for inspiration and
enlightenment. They may seek an ascetic life and, in the face
of suffering, transcend adversity with unbending faith and
conviction. Believers often inspire others with their courage
and determination and many, such as Mahatma Gandhi and
Martin Luther King, Jr., become leaders of political

movements. The confidence and determination of charismatic religious leaders often attract more followers than do their mystical truths of faith.

Believers who dedicate their lives to others do so with a conviction that transcends the vicissitudes of fortune and the tragedies of human fate. They may summon the courage to persevere when others would falter. The Dalai Lama, for instance, has endured exile from his homeland of Tibet since 1959, and throughout this time he has remained steadfast in his faith.

Whether they base their beliefs on religious doctrine or political ideology, devout believers are freed from the baggage of doubt. Hitler's faith in Aryan supremacy and Stalin's faith in communism were not spiritual beliefs, but both were belief systems that arose within the domain of Mystica and were, therefore, resistant to criticism.

In contrast to believers, *skeptics* confidently reject revealed truth. Nineteenth-century American skeptic Robert G. Ingersoll drew crowds to theaters across the U.S. with his knowledge, eloquence, and attacks on religious faith, such as: "There can be but little liberty on earth while men worship a tyrant in heaven."

Pure skeptics—people who reject all truths of faith, revelations, mysticism, and supernatural spirits—are rare. Even avowed atheists who reject traditional religious beliefs may still hold spiritual beliefs based in personal experience, or become deists who believe that a supernatural force set the universe in motion, and the experience of consciousness may cause staunch skeptics to leave room for the possibility of an invisible human spirit.

Richard Dawkins and Sam Harris come close to being pure skeptics. Dawkins, author and biologist, and Harris, author and physiologist, are unequivocal in condemning belief in spirits, but they do not reject the notion that there is a nonphysical aspect to each person—that is, a conscious mind. In *The End of Faith* (2005), Harris says there is a "conceptual gulf" between our consciousness and the physical world. Dawkins seems less eager to place consciousness outside the physical world, but in *The God Delusion* (2006) he did say that Julian Jayne's book, *The Origin of Consciousness in the Breakdown of the Bicameral Mind* (1976) was: "...either complete rubbish, or a work of consummate genius...." A more resolute skeptic might not have been so tolerant of Jayne's philosophical speculations about the transpatial nature of the conscious mind.

It is noteworthy that those who believe in God often redefine the skeptic's disbelief as a form of belief, specifically, the "belief" that there is no God. Obviously, this is word confusion or trickery, a rhetorical ploy designed to reframe the skeptic's doubts as beliefs. But *disbelief* cannot honestly be called *belief*. The rejection of faith does not constitute a faith. In his three-part video series titled "A Brief History of Disbelief" (PBS, 2007), British humorist, theater and opera director, and physician, Jonathan Miller explained his disapproval of the word *atheism*, saying that the word seems to suggest a more active position than is true in his case. Furthermore labeling skeptics as *atheists*—literally *not theists*—makes about as much sense as calling those who believe in God *askeptics*, that is, *not skeptics*.

Logica: Rationalists vs. Sophists

Rationalists live in a world of language and symbols, striving to determine which conclusions are validly inferred and which are not. Based on intuitive and logically derived propositions, they draw reasoned inferences. The natural occupation for rationalists is as scholarly writers and teachers. They happily spend their days organizing their knowledge and understanding into logically tight systems.

Historically, the critics of rationalists are *sophists,* scholars who understand the methods of reason but place their trust in the cultural ethos and public debate. Sophists present logic as a game, rather than an inerrant path to truth, and argue that the ordinary man's common sense is the proper measure of all things. "I am no slave to logic," the sophist might proudly assert, but like rationalists they tend to choose professions in academia.

Rationalists may accuse sophists of rejecting the search for truth, but the sophist does search for truth—just not in Logica. Sophists from Protagoras to Jacques Derrida, a twentieth century leader of the deconstructionist movement, took refuge in Rhetorica, where they found the tools to criticize the truths of reason.

Empirica: Realists vs. Idealists

Realists, the purists of Empirica, generally spend their days learning facts about a limited aspect of nature or history, delving into narrow specializations: the social life of ants, perception, climate change, black holes, World War I, or the life of a historical figure such as Galileo or George Washington. Realists have little time for politics, religion, or philosophy. It isn't that they reject the truths of other domains, only that they tend to see the methods of other domains as insufficient for establishing facts of nature and history. Realists learn what research findings show, and if an assertion is made without supportive research results, they may lose interest.

Empirica's strongest opponents are *idealists* who argue that the facts of reality cannot be known. They claim that we can know only our own experiences, not the things we experience. They argue that we understand our experiences through reasoned analysis, and they may, rather derisively, label a researcher's observations of the empirical world as naïve realism.

Even Plato reasoned that an account of perceived reality could never be more than a likely story. Over the centuries, idealists have echoed Plato's views by criticizing researchers who seek to describe reality and provide the factual truths of nature. The most radical anti-realists are the *solipsists*, thinkers who claim that we each live in a world made up of one experiencing mind, with no certainty that the physical world actually exists. Since the days of the pre-Socratic Gorgias, there have been philosophers who, paradoxically, doubt the very existence of the realists with whom they argue.

Dual-Domain Personalities

While each of us may have a preferred domain, few of us limit our pursuit of truth to a single domain. Many people do, however, habitually confine their search to two domains and largely ignore the truths of the two remaining domains.

Dual-domain truth seekers usually work well with people who share their domain preferences, but tend to be disinterested in the views of their complements—that is, people who prefer the other two domains. Dual-domain personalities can be grouped into three complementary pairs, to which we will assign the following labels:

TRUSTED DOMAINS	PERSONALITY
Rhetorica and Mystica	*Proselytizer*
Logica and Empirica	*Analyzer*
Empirica and Mystica	*Authority*
Rhetorica and Logica	*Questioner*
Mystica and Logica	*Traditionalist*
Rhetorica and Empirica	*Pragmatist*

Each of the three complementary pairs of personalities identified in the table above lack common ground for agreement, but this does not necessarily keep them from being attracted to each other. As my wise but cynical mother-in-law once said, "There are two kinds of people, and they tend to marry each other." And when they do, they disagree about almost everything.

Proselytizers vs. Analyzers

Proselytizers defend their faith or ideology with rhetoric, trusting their "gut feelings" or common sense, and minimizing any prediction based on an analysis of facts. High-profile proselytizers include doctrinaire political advocates and Christian evangelists who devote their lives to promoting their beliefs. The pastor of the largest church in North America, Joel S. H. Osteen, exemplifies the religious proselytizer. His strong Christian beliefs motivated him to develop extraordinary skills of persuasion, which allowed him to attract over 40,000 people to his weekly sermons and millions to his TV program.

Those of us who observe political life in Washington, DC, were fascinated several years ago by the marriage of Mary Matalin and James Carville, attack dogs of the Republican and Democratic parties, respectively. Matalin and Carville are on opposing teams, playing the same game. Friendship between such dedicated political advocates must be based on respect for competitors who work in the same two domains. While their political values and motives may be at opposite poles, their rhetorical tactics and commitment to political ideology make them compatible; and luckily, neither married an analyzer, whom they would most likely have found unbearably tedious and tentative.

Analyzers reason from facts and are ideally suited to professions in applied science, such as medicine and engineering. Their success in these analytical professions depends not only upon grasping facts, but also on reasoning without errors. To solve physical problems, engineers reason with exacting care from physical facts, just as physicians reason from biological facts. Analyzers have little interest in the opinions and beliefs of proselytizers. They are problem-solvers who spend their days on rational and factual matters, and they are often perplexed by the endless and seemingly pointless ideological disagreements and religious disputes that swirl around them. Although they are typically slow to take up arms in wars based on religious or ideological beliefs, they can serve on either side as strategists and problem solvers.

Authorities vs. Questioners

Authorities know the facts and know what they believe, and thereby have the confidence and presumption to lead others. Before each military mission, officers go over a battle plan based on the facts as they are known, and then may lead the troops in prayer. No general enters gladly into battle without the gods and the facts squarely on his side. Authorities also make good coaches. They approach games in the same way that generals approach battles, with a plan based on the facts and a prayer based on faith.

Coaches and generals make use of questioners, but they stop the questioning once they commit to a plan. Once the planned action is underway, they cannot allow questioners to waste time raising doubt and sapping morale. Halftime interviews with coaches often result in the same response, "We are going to stick with our game plan, but we need to execute better." The halftime break is only long enough to encourage and motivate the team, so questioning the game plan is rarely permitted.

Questioners reason from opinions and are attracted to occupations involving problem solving in human affairs, such as administrative positions and jobs that require frequent committee meetings. Questioners neither proselytize for their faith, nor demand acceptance of the facts of science or history, but they are adept at identifying differences of opinion and following the logic of complex arguments. Unlike authorities, questioners rarely rise to positions of leadership, but when they do, they seldom gain the loyalty of those who work for them. On the other hand, questioners usually excel in positions that require skills in moderating disputes. Kofi Annan, former Secretary General of the United Nations, provides an excellent example of a questioner who rose to the top by mastering the art of diplomacy.

Traditionalists vs. Pragmatists

Traditionalists defend their faith with reason. They know what they believe and are able to provide rational support for their beliefs. The obvious example of the traditionalist is the theologian, but there are also traditionalists who apply logical analysis to political ideologies. The religious historian and theologian Elaine Pagels and the historian, journalist, and political commentator Jon Meacham are among the outstanding American traditionalists of our time. Successful traditionalists tend to have a strong moral compass and may become influential and respected members of society, but they are unlikely to find common understanding or agreement with their complement, the pragmatist.

Pragmatists defend their opinions with the facts. They do well in work that requires an appreciation for facts, as well as a willingness to consider everyone's opinion. They are attracted to practical occupations in such fields as investments, advertising, sales, or marketing—including the marketing of political candidates. Pragmatists easily learn the facts and persuade others of the real or imagined benefits to be had from their services, products, or proposals. Unlike traditionalists, pragmatists often show little interest in traditional values or ethical standards.

Eclectics and Nihilists

Beyond the personality types made up by single-domain purists, critics, and dual-domain personalities, there are *Eclectics* who accept the truths of all four domains. These four-domain personalities may possess the intellectual flexibility to move smoothly from one domain to another, guided only by the form and context of each assertion under consideration. At their best, they compartmentalize the truths of the four domains, tolerating without complaint the inevitable contradictions between domains.

Eclectics' broad range of understanding and tolerance for the views of others make them well suited for careers in management. Well-read American political leaders such as President John F. Kennedy and President Barack Obama tended to choose as their advisors the "best and the brightest," eclectics who had mastered the rules of all four domains and were rightly considered to be intellectuals.

Unfortunately, most eclectics are not intellectual, they are just people who casually shift from one domain to another, without discipline or clear understanding or awareness. They frequently confuse themselves about what is true, and they confuse others. Not surprisingly, these less-disciplined eclectics function best in work settings that provide enforced structure and routine, and to their credit, they successfully fill many of the mid-level positions that make the wheels of commerce and government turn. For better or for worse, this personality type makes up the largest part of modern society.

The complement of the eclectic is the *nihilist*. To nihilists, the search for truth is a fool's errand, so they contemptuously reject the methods and truths of all four domains. Nihilists tend to be attracted to creative occupations such as art and literature.

Informed nihilists may be found at the center of social life, and in the lead when anarchy reigns. They are skilled in discrediting all assertions of truth and disrespecting those who make the assertions. In this post-truth era the doors have opened wide for nihilists to rise to dictatorial power by making demagogic assertions and strategically attacking inconvenient truths of all four domains. The forty-fifth President of the United States, Donald John Trump, is perhaps the most successful nihilist of our times. Oddly, his most ardent supporters are credulous eclectics. As has been widely noted, politics makes strange bedfellows.

Although no one is a pure nihilist, some young truth-seekers walk this heady path and, for a time, meet the criteria for, and earn the label of, *nihilist*. A few remain nihilists for life, and if they are ever elected to a position of leadership, a democracy can quickly descend into autocracy.

Personality Traits

Categorical terms should never be allowed to obscure individual uniqueness, intellectual flexibility, or our tendency to grow and change. Each of us embodies a unique and complex personality that cannot be replicated or boxed in with a label. Most of us begin our search as eclectics, but may later distinguish and organize our personality by what we reject. Eventually, we become known for the personality traits revealed by the paths we take in search of truth.

We may intentionally reveal our personalities by the way we defend the methods of one or another domain of truth. A particularly devout person might, for example, habitually use revealing expressions such as "praise the Lord" or "God willing," but most of us are unlikely to display the nature of our search for truth quite so overtly. Asked to tell about ourselves, we tend to avoid discussions that expose our domain biases, but people who know us best know our personalities are composed of a well-established array of preferences and habits, and chief among these are the paths we choose to follow in the search of truth.

9

Truth, Language, and Information

SOMEWHERE ALONG THE long evolutionary journey of life, there appeared a species of primates that walked upright, with hands and arms free to make gestures—to indicate the way to food, to signal the direction of approaching danger—and most importantly, possessing the ability to learn the relation of gestures to objects and events. These social primates were our ancestors, and their culture-specific gestures were the earliest form of *referential communication*—that is, the psychological act of referring others to specific things and events (Kantor, 1977; Gardner, 1987).

Referring was by no means the first form of communication. Social cues—such as fear cries, threatening postures, and mating calls—provide the reflexive communications that coordinate the interactions of all animal species. These cues can be as simple as a hatchling's chirp or as complicated as a mating dance, but however complex the cues may be, their functions remain quite simple: to facilitate social interactions essential, or once essential, to the evolution and survival of the species.

Early hominids went beyond social cueing and evolved an entirely new culture-specific form of communication, allowing them to deliberately direct the attention of members of their culture to specific objects or events in the immediate physical world. Over the millennia, this *referring* gradually expanded to include reference to things in the past, in the future, or to things far away.

Referring was an essential element for the development of a multitude of human skills, from day-to-day cooperation in locating food sources or identifying dangers, to recalling the past and planning the future. This new *communication about things*—that is, human *language*—provided the complex form of communication necessary for the transfer of cultural knowledge and understanding from one generation to the next, and allowed children to learn and expand on knowledge acquired by previous generations.

Origins of Language

Because referential gesturing, the earliest form of referring, required visual contact and free hands, it was increasingly augmented and then largely replaced by vocalizations. But from that early time until today, gestures remain a part of referential language. When we need to communicate with people who do not speak our language or can't hear us, we revert to pointing and representational gestures.

In early childhood many deaf children are taught a formal and elaborate manual language. In the United States, American Sign Language is the standard, although some deaf children, especially those who lose their hearing after beginning to speak, as well as those who retain some hearing abilities, are often taught speech and lip-reading skills.

Over many thousands of years, human speech grew increasingly complex, gradually incorporating the terminology needed to communicate techniques for building shelters, creating garments, cooking and storing food, and coordinating relationships and village defenses. Because language is culture-specific, groups isolated from one another developed different languages. As a consequence, explanations and understanding evolved along a different path for each linguistic group. Each group developed a vocabulary tailored to specific features of the local environment and to its cultural history.

In stable village cultures, terms for dwellings and tool construction developed rapidly, whereas in nomadic cultures, complex vocabularies for weather conditions and terrain grew more rapidly. Nonetheless, individuals who happened to experience more than one culture could learn multiple languages and provide communication links for intercultural transfer of understanding.

The Spoken Truth

Spoken language was the medium through which members of early cultures described when, where, and how events had occurred or would occur, providing a common understanding that held villages and cultural groups together. Early humans told and retold stories, amassing a tribal lore through which each individual's understanding was expanded. Stories that described mating and birth provided primitive accounts of the creation of human life. By detailing the specifics of individual suffering and dying, stories provided the first understanding of the relationships among injury, sickness, and death.

Oral traditions grew into authorized, accepted, and enduring descriptions and explanations, and formed the first truths of each culture. The earliest assertions of truths were advanced through repetition and persuasive arguments. Early humans debated what was or was not the case, repeating the process over and over. When disagreements occurred, individuals attempted to persuade others to accept their descriptions and accounts of events, just as we do today. Children heard the conversations and debates swirling around them, and they rapidly acquired the rhetorical truths of their culture.

Human understanding traveled more-or-less effortlessly across time, with each generation adding its own experiences and explanations. When the intergenerational transfer of truth was broken, understanding was lost, but because human infants have such a long period of dependency on parents, cultural understanding remained stable across generations. Rhetorical truths evolved slowly, accommodating the changing conditions and growth in understanding of each generation.

This powerful medium for communication and education set the stage for what is arguably the greatest shift in the entire history of evolution. *As spoken truth advanced, humans gained the understanding essential for reshaping their environment, rather than just evolving to fit it.* For the last 100,000 years or more, human survival has depended on learning how to modify human environments.

Humans reversed the direction of the evolutionary process. Instead of just being altered by environmental forces, they began to alter their environment to suit their needs, building shelters, constructing tools, sewing hides, weaving containers, cultivating fruits and vegetables, and cooking and preserving food. The survival value brought by their unique communication abilities, and the rhetorical truths that these abilities conveyed to the next generation, cannot be overstated. *Cultural evolution became far faster and more consequential than biological evolution.*

The debated truths of Rhetorica were not, however, the only truths that guided early human cultures. Those individuals who best knew the truths of the culture were of greatest value to the group, and they became respected leaders and teachers. In solemn ceremonies involving symbols and rituals, they recited essential truths, and warned their followers not to doubt or question the honored truths thus revealed. From these authorized truths, the formal religions of Mystica would one day emerge; but before that could happen, another step in the evolution of language would be required.

The Written Truth

Surprisingly, written language did not evolve directly from spoken language. Instead, linguistic symbols grew from representational drawings denoting animals, people, foods, and other things. Tribal stories were recorded in drawings and these drawings gradually evolved over centuries into strings of pictographic symbols, and then into cryptic symbols, or *ideographs*. While it was easy to learn to interpret the early pictographic drawings, only trained scribes were able to understand ideographic symbols and to read the texts that were created by stringing these symbols together.

Unwritten assertions of truth had long been passed along by word of mouth. From village to village and generation to generation, stories evolved naturally as new interpretations and understandings gained credibility. But with the advent of written symbols, oral stories and assertions could be recorded and thereby standardized across generations. These symbolized stories took on an almost magical permanence in each culture.

Scribes immortalized the glories of leaders and heroes, and commemorated great hunts, feasts, and battles. The resulting texts were often literally written in stone, and passed relatively unchanged and undisputed from one generation to the next. The written word's power and resistance to revision were most apparent to leaders who, as a matter of course, began to employ scribes to record their achievements, tax receipts, and laws. Some of these writings would endure to become the foundational truths of Western Civilization.

As scribes learned to symbolize objects, events, and ideas, they found a secondary and much more flexible use for their symbols. They discovered that they could symbolize speech sounds. In time, these new *phonetic symbols* were expanded and organized into alphabets that allowed verbatim recordings of oral traditions.

Alphabetic writing dates back at least to the twelfth century BCE when the Proto-Canaanite alphabet evolved from Egyptian hieroglyphs. The first alphabets provided symbols for only consonant sounds, but they were later enlarged to include vowels. These first phonetic alphabets provided the foundation for the creation of alphabets for the spoken languages of other cultures.

Early truths of the Western World were recorded in Hebrew, Greek, or Latin alphabetic characters. The truths of the Jewish scribes were recorded in Hebrew, the truths of Greek philosophers were recorded in Greek, and the truths Roman scholars and clerics were recorded in Latin.

In ancient cultures, the influence of the written word was limited not only by the availability of texts, but also by the rarity of literacy. Scribes became the scholarly elites of their cultures, and the books over which they labored, often for years, were prized, protected, and housed in libraries accessible only to a select few.

The power of the written word became the basis for, and the sustaining force of, truths of faith. Scribes who maintained temple and monastery libraries controlled a new type of truth, infallible truths that were not to be questioned but accepted as final and absolute. Some of these truths were eventually presented as the words of gods or their prophets.

As scribes standardized rules of grammar and syntax, written language took on an orderliness and clarity of meaning not found in ordinary speech. Many scribes read widely, comparing and contrasting written documents and texts, and judging whether there were agreements or contradictions. In the context of this growing demand for clarity and consistency of language, Greek scholars pioneered a new form of truth based on analysis of the compatibility and incompatibility of assertions. Greek philosophers from Thales to Aristotle elaborated a system of logical and mathematical analysis that allowed them to assess the validity of assertions, establishing a new search for truth through rational debate and logical analysis.

The Eastern World had been slow to adopt phonetic writings. In the twentieth century, Chinese phonetic symbols, *Zhuyin* (commonly called *"Bopomofo"*), began to augment traditional ideographic symbols. Ideographic symbols are still a central part of written language in China, Japan, Korea, and other eastern countries, and western cultures also retained ideographic symbols for special purposes, such as mathematics, musical notation, and signs. Ideographic symbols must be read for meaning rather than sound, so regardless of readers' spoken language, they can learn to interpret or "read" the meaning of ideographic symbols and to translate them into their spoken language.

The Printed Truth

The earliest books had been painstakingly reproduced with quill pens and brushes. In China in the first millennium printed texts emerged. In Europe, the second millennium, saw the development of mechanical printing presses, speeding up the process and insuring consistency in reprinting. In the middle of the fifteenth century, written language underwent a huge transformation when Johannes Gutenberg, a printer in Mainz, Germany, devised a system of movable type that made printing faster and easier. Instead of carving letters and symbols into a wooden printing plate, or casting metal printing plates to print each page of text, Gutenberg set pre-cast and moveable metal type into grooves on a blank plate. This new typesetting technology greatly increased the efficiency of the mechanical printing process, allowing fast and easy reproduction of books. Bibles and other important texts were soon available in libraries throughout Europe.

The moveable-type press promoted the spread of literacy and ignited a revolution in religion and education. It might be too strong to say that the Protestant Reformation was a direct result of the printing revolution that Gutenberg started, but it is otherwise hard to imagine such a rapid spread of the Protestant movement. As Bibles became accessible to more readers, independent interpretations of the scriptures inevitably led to the questioning of the authority of the Pope. The first Gutenberg Bible was available by 1455, and only sixty-two years later Martin Luther is reputed to have tacked his Ninety-Five Theses to the door of the Wittenberg Castle Church, thus igniting a Christian rebellion that led to the Protestant Reformation.

Scholarly books on religion, philosophy, and science became more accessible, and an unprecedented advance in education and understanding swept across the Western world. By the end of the seventeenth century, scholars in Europe and beyond had gained access to printed works by ancient scholars as well as contemporaries such as Francis Bacon, René Descartes, Isaac Newton, and other great thinkers and researchers of the day.

In the eighteenth century, libraries around the world acquired large arrays of books on religion, philosophy, history, geography, science, and medicine. Human understanding had begun to move forward at the speed of the printing press. Books were readily available to a growing audience of international scholars and researchers, and secular education began to emerge from the shadows of Christianity, spreading across Europe and on to the colonies. Even private homes of the wealthy featured book collections presenting the truths of Rhetorica, Mystica, Logica, and Empirica.

By the second half of the nineteenth century, with mechanized printing presses widely available, weekly and then daily newspapers were published in most of the world's cities. Early journalists tended to focus on local political and social activities, but they also reported important or spectacular events at the regional, national, and international levels. Regular printing deadlines necessitated a writing style that was simple, fresh, and superficial, and many of these early newspapers lacked rigorous editorial standards and were open to exaggerations, inaccuracies and editorial bias.

Regardless of their shortcomings, independent newspapers were destined to become the voice of community life, and of the democratic process of government. In their pages, the disputed as well as the accepted news of the day was updated and published on a weekly and eventually daily basis.

The Transmitted Truth

The approach of the twentieth century brought great advances in science and a plethora of new technologies, including those that made it easier to record events and to disseminate information. Photography emerged as the standard method for documenting important places and events, and telegraph lines provided rapid cross-country and even trans-Atlantic transmission of information. As the nineteenth century ended, available information technologies included phonographs, wireless telegraphs, telephones, and motion pictures. Ordinary citizens were no doubt in awe of all this new communication technology, and quite sure that every possible communication device had been invented. In 1899, Charles H. Duell, Commissioner of Office of U.S. Patents, urged President William McKinley to abolish the office, saying "Everything that can be invented has been invented" (Cerf and Navasky, 1998). The first half of the twentieth century brought many more inventions that advanced communications; among these were radios, magnetic recording machines, and televisions.

By 1955, homes in modern urban and suburban settings were equipped with radios, phonographs, telephones, and televisions. Tape recorders, transistor radios, and color televisions soon followed. By the last quarter of the twentieth century, businesses, governmental agencies, and colleges had grown dependent on copiers, fax machines, electronic calculators, mainframe computers, and videocassette recorders. But all these technologies were soon eclipsed as personal computers made their way into schools, businesses, and homes throughout the developed world, their speed and capacity nearly doubling with each passing year. Luggable computers shrank to portable and then to notebook and now palm size, while computing power, screen resolution, printer speed, and battery life steadily increased.

Cell phone systems were growing, and by the Nineties they had become essential in many professions. The size of cell phones decreased steadily and cell towers sprang up along major highways and around urban centers. By the start of the twenty-first century, personal computers were almost as common as televisions, and all professionals were presumed to have cell phones. Over the next twenty years, cell phones became smart phones, a ubiquitous device for personal auditory and visual communication around the world.

In the first decade of the new century, the internet blossomed into an ever-expanding, multi-indexed, information and communication system. Cable and satellite television brought hundreds of channels and around-the-clock news and entertainment. By the end of first decade of the new millennium, each smart phone served as computer, alarm clock, audio recorder, video camera, global positioning system, scheduler, address book, appointment reminder, calculator, internet access system, photo album, music library, email transmitting and receiving device, video game player, and much more. More importantly, they allowed almost instantaneous voice, video, and text communication around the world.

Searching for Truth in a Sea of Information

With all the progress in communication technology, we might think the search for truth has been the beneficiary. In fact, *truth* became more elusive, as we occupied ourselves with gathering unvetted information and passing it along.

Consider the example of information disseminated about the attack on the World Trade Center in New York City on September 11, 2001. In his book, *The Assault on Reason* (2007), Al Gore states that six years after the attack nearly half the American public still believed that Iraq's Saddam Hussein was involved with the attack. With all the information available, and from so many different sources, we must wonder how the public was so thoroughly uninformed. The answer is that they were not uninformed. They were more informed than ever before, but they found it increasingly difficult to decide what was false and what was true.

The essential facts about the events of 9/11 were not easily identified in the mass of information on the subject. We were told that Saddam Hussein was responsible for the attack, and we were told that he was not; we were told that the CIA arranged the attack, that the hijackers could not have slipped through the CIA's security systems, that the buildings could not have been brought down without planted explosives, and that Jews knew in advance to stay away from the World Trade Center on that fateful day. We were also provided information on al-Qaeda and details about the identity, recruitment, and training of individual hijackers, their methods of entry into the United States, the FBI's failure to act on that information, an analysis of the structural failures of the buildings, and particulars about the people who perished that day.

With all this information and much more, the problem was certainly not a lack of information. The problem was that most people did not limit their search to the facts established through diligent research. Instead, they collected whatever information they found, decided for themselves what was true, and disregarded the fact that what they found was mostly propaganda, rumor, and speculation. As a consequence, what people accepted as true was largely a reflection of their personal fears, hopes, biases, and limited understanding.

In his book, Gore suggests that through personal powers of reasoning we can each discover the truth for ourselves, but analyses of the facts surrounding the events of 9/11 were already available. The problem was that most people treated research findings and logical inferences as just more information, no better and no worse than popular opinions and personal beliefs.

Is the problem just that we have become passive television watchers and internet surfers, disinterested in research and reasoned discourse? No. The situation is really worse than that. We collect information from television, print, and the internet with no regard for which test of truth—if any—that information has passed or failed. Then we attempt to reason our way through the disorderly mass of information and accept as true those items that fit our personal biases and level of understanding.

In this new millennium, we find all four domains of truth in serious trouble. The Information Age opened a Pandora's box of unedited, untested, uncensored assertions that now spread rapidly around the world, overwhelming and supplanting established truth. Rhetorica's rules of formal public debate have given way to talk-show shouting matches, partisan blogs, deliberate misinformation, and sensationalized news reports. Mystica's established traditions of faith have been replaced by religious docudramas, New Age spiritualism, televised mega-church preachers, and freelancing internet theologians. In the institutions of Logica, information collected from the internet and from television is rapidly replacing carefully edited textbooks and logical lectures and essays. Rather than search out Empirica's scientific experiments and historical studies, students learn science and history from internet sites, and trust that they are receiving the truths of Empirica. It is now a popular goal to have internet access available to every child in every classroom and home, so students will be rapidly exposed to a mix of reliable and unreliable information.

Truth has become a needle in the haystack of information. We no longer have time for formal debate and polite persuasion, for scholarly study of religious doctrines, for rational analysis of virtually anything, or for learning the methods and facts of science and history. What we accept as true is generally no more than unvetted information we chanced to encounter and personally deemed to be true. The word *truth* rarely enters our conversation, except to mean not a lie. We cannot keep track of the sources of the information we gather, and when we have doubts about its reliability, we simply collect more information.

Our problem is not that truth is inaccessible. Materials from the archives of Rhetorica, Mystica, Logica, and Empirica are readily available through the internet—along with the millions of sites that supply untested and uncensored assertions. No internet search engines have been designed to exclude assertions that have not been validated in one of the four domains. That would, after all, exclude all but a tiny fraction of the information now available. That said, Wikipedia provides information that is at least vetted by editors.

So, the Information Express roars into the twenty-first century, destination unknown. We each have a one-way ticket and a seat by the window; we are going somewhere together, at a faster and faster pace. Where are we heading? Should we try to slow down, to return to the search for truth, or must we all speed onward, gathering more and more unvetted information?

Because the internet allows individuals to post reactions to what they read, information gatherers such as Al Gore can think that the internet can take us back to the reasoned discourse prevalent at the founding of our democracy. But, sadly, such optimism is unwarranted. The fact that the internet allows individual commentary does not mean it promotes civil debate or reasoned discourse; rather, it facilitates the spread and multiplication of untested assertions.

So long as we fail to respect and differentiate the four domains of truth, searches of the internet will always result in vastly more unvetted information than established truth from the four domains. Our daily decisions—as students, producers, parents, consumers, and voters—will be increasingly based on disinformation and unreliable information. The real question is not how can we return to reasoned and orderly public discourse, but how we can stop gathering information and focus on the search for truth, a search that begins with identifying the institutions, archives, and methods of the four domains.

10

Truth in the Information Age

HUMAN SURVIVAL DEPENDS upon our ability to predict changes, and with our dizzying rate of innovation, forecasting events in the twenty-first century presents a special challenge. The speed of technological and social change makes the future a constantly moving target. To avoid disasters in this new century, we need to be able to make critical decisions quickly and accurately. Even when armed with the truths of reason and research, we still cannot predict very far into the future. By the time we see a problem looming, it is often too late to change course.

Consider the question of climate change: If we project the current warming trend to continue into the future, we have little time to avert disasters in the form of rising ocean levels, increases in storm severity, changes in weather patterns, forest fires, and crop failures. If the changes that have occurred over recent years are nothing more than cyclical fluctuations in the normal conditions of the earth, there may be no need to take action. But if we take a wait-and-see approach, we clearly risk losing critical time needed to correct the problem or to prepare to live with cataclysmic environmental changes.

The specific domains of truth that we trust will influence which decisions we make about climate change. If we choose Rhetorica, the ensuing public debate is likely to become entangled in political considerations, rather than remaining an honest debate about established facts. If we choose Mystica, climate changes may be attributed to God's plan. But if the methods and truths of Logica and Empirica are consulted, we may·soon have essential facts and logical predictions for a clear plan of action. Action by democracies would still rely, however, on the outcome of time-consuming political debate.

When making personal decisions, some people may choose a fifth option: reject the rules of all four domains, and demand to have transcendent truth—truth not tethered to one of the four domains. They may seek truth independent of the limitations of cultural traditions for testing assertions.

Searching for Transcendent Truth

Some very intelligent people attempt to escape the boundaries of the four domains, hoping to find transcendent truth—that is, truth that extends beyond all restrictions of method and time. In Robert M. Pirsig's autobiographical work *Zen and the Art of Motorcycle Maintenance* (1974), his alter ego Phaedrus attempts to escape the bounds of the four domains. Pirsig writes that Phaedrus "...was just drifting...looking at lateral truth....", unable to follow any known method because the "methods and procedures...were all screwed up in the first place."

Phaedrus searched for a graduate program that would not limit his search for truth, and settled on an interdisciplinary program titled "Analysis of Ideas and Study of Methods," at the University of Chicago. He soon discovered, however, that some of the faculty members with whom he would be working were petty, so he drifted again, still seeking escape from the limitations of traditional methods.

Instead of transcendent truth, what Phaedrus found was insanity, a world beyond true and false, where no rules of truth apply. He received psychiatric treatment, and eventually returned to a more cautious search for truth, but with a new personality. Phaedrus was gone. Pirsig had become a more restrained person who reminded himself frequently that his search for truth must remain within the bounds of order and sanity.

Most people who search for truth beyond the four domains do not drift into insanity, but they do delude themselves. By refusing to accept the limitations of truths and methods of the four domains, they subscribe to the delusion that their personal search can reveal transcendent truth—truth pure and self-evident. They convince themselves and each other that they can personally know the truth when they see it. What they are actually doing is placing their faith in personal insights.

Searching for Personal Truth

Scholars often present the search for truth as a personal affair, free from the methods and restraints of the four domains. Some even lament that this personal search cannot be freed from the mental limits of language.

In his book *Truth: A History and a Guide for the Perplexed* (1997), Felipe Fernández-Armesto (a historian who occupied chairs at Tufts University and the University of London before joining the History Department at the University of Notre Dame in 2009) proposed four types of personal truths: the truths we feel, the truths we learn from others, the truths we personally think up, and the truths we perceive through our senses. These four psychological sources provide us, he says, with the truths we come to accept; and in Fernández-Armesto's view, these personal truths are, unfortunately, "imprisoned by language." He laments that there is no means for framing objective reality outside the limits of language, which makes it impossible to access objective reality.

Fernández-Armesto is right: We know no higher experience than human experience, no higher understanding than human understanding, and no truth higher than that formed within the confines of, and expressed with, language or symbols. Moreover, in order for personally accepted "truths" to be tested and established in one of the four domains, they must first be asserted—that is, expressed in some linguistic or symbolic form.

We cannot publicly assess the indescribable truths of experiences until they are confined to the linguistic order imposed by public expression, but this in no way diminishes the personal value of sudden flashes of understanding or fleeting clarity of perception. For example, we may feel that we finally understand the true source of happiness, but if we attempt to express such insights in words, we risk distorting and losing the prized insight. And yet, taking that risk is an essential step toward establishing a new truth within one of the four traditional domains. Unarticulated understanding, knowledge, and appreciation—however valuable and inspiring to the individual—can't replace or even challenge the public search for truth through the four domains.

"Ah," the guru says, "the wisdom I could impart to you if only we could communicate without words." But the only way to escape language is to stop asking and answering. To escape the order of language, we must eliminate every linguistic structure of our thinking and understanding. And if we succeed and escape the orderly confines of language, we risk entering a world without order, the world that Pirsig's Phaedrus found, the confusing, dead-end world in which we believe our untethered personal experience provides ultimate truth.

Truths discovered through personal experience are at best assertions of truth not yet validated by the methods of any domain. To find known truth, we must select from the established truths of the four domains, and use the language of these truths to assess and frame the knowledge gained through our experience.

Protecting Truth

A free press is the mark of a democracy, and its absence identifies a regime that regulates truth for political ends. To consolidate their control over truth, authoritarian leaders enact laws designed to regulate the methods of all four domains. Tyrants, despots, and dictators understand intuitively that the first step in controlling people is to control their search for truth, and they accomplish this by limiting public debate, establishing a state religion, curbing academic freedom, restricting research, flooding the internet with barrages of unvetted assertions, and presenting themselves as the only reliable source of truth. Does this sound familiar?

From the beginning of civilization until the eighteenth century, no human society enjoyed anything that approached the freedom of expression we enjoy today. Only in the twentieth century did secular democracies rise to prominence on the world stage and encourage a free and open search for truth. Yet many of the world's peoples still live in police states or theocratic nations where open expression of the truths of the four domains is dangerous.

While the veil of communism has been lifted in Eastern Europe, in the remaining communist countries—China, Cuba, and North Korea—leaders generally hold a tight rein on the search for truth. But elsewhere, the rise of democracy has brought a golden age in the search for truth.

The relatively unrestricted search for truth in the United States deserves special comment since it was here, over 200 years ago, that, arguably, the first secular, constitutional democracy was introduced to the modern world. In recent years, truth's newest enemy has taken root and flourished here in "the land of the free." The increased flow of information, facilitated by advances in communication technology, has consumed us, leaving us with little time to search for truth and thus open to manipulation by populists and autocratic leaders. We are proud when our children demonstrate a talent for electronic information gathering, but when it comes to understanding the methods and truths of the four domains, our pride must be moderated by their general lack of ability to discriminate among opinion, belief, inference, and fact. They tend to treat all assertions as information. The question remains, will citizens of all democracies around the world continue to seek competence in the search for truth in the four domains, or will they settle for the lesser skills of information gathering?

Are Truths Converging?

The tests of truth in each domain are relatively stable, so we might presume that the truths within each of the four domains are trending toward agreement and compatibility.

That is what we find in Logica and Empirica, but in Rhetorica and Mystica we find a trend is toward accommodation of disagreement.

Convergence within Domains

In *Rhetorica*, truths converge and diverge as a natural consequence of cultural evolution and culture clashes. While debate and persuasion reduce differences on some issues, they bring divergence on others. In fact, vigorous debate seems more likely to exacerbate partisan disagreement than to produce a general agreement.

Political disagreements in some democracies have, in recent times, grown more entrenched and hostile. This is seen by many as a trend rather than a cyclical change, although after 9/11 American politicians, fearful of attack from abroad, rallied together and were supported by other democracies around the world. For a few months, it seemed that democracies were destined for an era of cooperation, but then the political accord ended almost as abruptly as it began, with democratically elected leaders debating the wisdom of attacking Iraq. The return of discord was perhaps inevitable. The methods of Rhetorica focus our attention on disagreements, more than on agreements.

In democracies, political disagreements can be resolved by vote, but sometimes leaders cannot agree on a method to resolve clashing opinions and the ultimate solution involves physical conflict. In the middle of the nineteenth century, conservative American politicians argued that slavery should be a matter of state law, while many liberals argued that human rights took precedence over state laws. The issue of slavery versus human rights could not be resolved by vote, so the result was a civil war.

In *Mystica*, the divergence of faiths, denominations, and cults has outpaced convergence. The recent announcement that "*United* Methodist Church is expected to *split*" is an example. Religious beliefs fluctuate with reinterpretation of doctrines, new revelations, and evolving cultural values, and the resulting doctrinal divisions are often enduring. The large number of Protestant denominations and unaffiliated Christian churches provides a measure of the tendency of beliefs and scriptural interpretations to diverge.

The history of Mystica documents the losing struggle to promote ecumenical agreement by accentuating compatible beliefs. Many wars have been fought between cultures with similar but conflicting systems of belief, and more are sure to come.

In *Logica*, scholars are bound by common logical methods that lead inexorably to widely accepted truths. Logica's rules often lead independent thinkers to the same conclusions more-or-less simultaneously, as when both Isaac Newton and Gottfried Wilhelm von Leibniz independently developed methods of calculus. This synchrony was neither a chance happening nor a miracle. As long as scholars adhere to the formal methods of reason, they tend to arrive at the same conclusions, and truths of reason naturally tend to converge.

In *Empirica*, convergence of truths is essential and inevitable. Charles Darwin prepared to explain the implications of his research findings just as Alfred Russel Wallace was preparing to publish an almost identical account of the data available to him at the time. In 1858 the two men jointly presented their findings to the Linnean Society. Such convergence of theories of nature are a product of the order that nature imposes on research findings. Convergence in Empirica's theories is inevitable because its truths reflect the enduring order observed in nature.

Convergence between Domains

It is not the conflicts within domains that pose the greatest threat to the search for agreement; it is the conflicts between domains. The four domains disagree on where truth is to be found and on how it is to be validated. Even though Logica and Empirica have found cooperation to be beneficial to both, they do not reach the same conclusions independently of each other. That is, their truths are not converging.

Mathematics arose in Logica, and physical laws arose in Empirica, but researchers could not have succeeded in discovering the physical laws of nature without mastering the methods of both domains. While logicians and mathematicians do not rely on scientific research to test their truths, and scientists do not accept theories of nature just because they are logically valid, each domain relies on truths of the other, so much so that they are often seen as a single unified domain.

Truths of the modern world of science clash with the old world's decreed truths of faith, threatening both worlds. As long as faith-inspired terrorist organizations are funded by autocratic and theocratic states, and democracies with advanced scientific understanding created vast armies equipped with the latest technology, accommodation between the truths of Mystica and the truths of the other domains seems to be an unrealistic hope.

We should not expect the four domains to somehow converge as they mature, and that lack of convergence will always necessitate accommodation of differences, if harmony and peace are to prevail. National leaders must recognize, understand, and accommodate the conflicts between domains, or else nations will always be preparing for the next war.

Every war the United States has entered since World War II has been shadowed by questions about the war's objective and the nation's exit strategy. Americans say they are fighting to end fighting, when in fact their conflicts with other governments and organizations are usually clashes between domains. Their actual objectives often seem to be the imposition of the methods of Rhetorica, Logica, and Empirica on theocratic and ideological states and organizations, and the establishment of freedom of, but not domination by, truths of Mystica.

Those countries the United States has opposed are historically authoritarian states headed by ideologues, theocrats, and militant dictators, leaders who do not allow freedom of belief or political expression. Ironically, many heads of state that the Americans have long supported also fit this profile.

Admiration for nationalists and authoritarian leaders has increased in recent years in many democratic nations, most notably the United States. It is a bit early to predict where this is leading, but we know from the first half of the twentieth century, when dictatorships emerged around the world, that democracies can disappear almost overnight. When that happens, all four domains of truth can be subjugated and exploited in order for a despotic leader to maintain dictatorial control.

The Information Age

Unruly debates, personal beliefs, irrational thinking, pseudoscience, and even deceit are spread by the information media with the same authority, freedom, and rapidity as is accorded to assertions that have passed a formal test of truth. We have entered the new millennium incessantly gathering unvetted information. We seem to presume that if we collect enough information we will find the truth, if it exists, and be able to recognize it when we see it. We have become information gatherers with only a modest understanding of, and respect for, the truths and methods of the four domains.

To gain an appreciation for how far modern civilization has traveled down the information highway, you might try this little exercise: Unplug your television, turn off your phone and radio, ignore newspapers and magazines, and avoid the internet. Take time to learn about a legislative process, a seminary's teachings, a liberal arts college's curriculum, and a research laboratory's daily functions. Go to a college library and read about a historic court decision, the history of a religious doctrine, a philosophical proposition from the Golden Age of Greece, or research methods and findings in a scientific research journal. In these activities you will encounter truths that stand in stark contrast to the mindless chatter of talk shows, sensationalized news reports, shrill warnings from the news media, and unruly shouting matches on cable television. You may see that our immersion in information gathering has led us away from the slow deliberations of rule-governed debate, comparisons of religious doctrines, methods of logical analysis, and findings of scientific and historical research. In short, our struggle to follow the daily flood of information has drawn us away from the four traditional paths to truth.

The choice is yours—or rather it is ours. Shall we return to the search for truth, or continue traveling down the neon highway of information? At no time in the history of human life has truth been more bountiful or mattered more than it does today, but as social and technological change continues to gather speed, it is more important than ever that we, as individuals, organizations, communities, and nations, handle our disagreements wisely and efficiently. Peaceful co-existence depends on our ability to recognize the source of our disagreements, and to achieve that, we must understand and respect the four domains of truth.

ACKNOWLEDGEMENTS

Nick Coulson, JoAnne Rains, Robert Koewing, Jim Krider, Richard Bond, Peggy Tilley, and Dee Leff offered encouragement and challenges that led to many improvements in the work that finally emerged. I am especially indebted to Jonathan Leff and to my wife G. P. Gardner, each of whom read the entire manuscript several times, provided many corrections, and noted areas that needed clarification or deletion. Without their help, advice, and support, the project would never have matured.

BIBLIOGRAPHY

Adler, Mortimer J. (1983) *How to Speak, How to Listen.* Macmillan, New York, NY.

Aristotle (see Roberts & Bywater, 1954; Jones, 1969; or Hett, 1975)

Balsiger, Dave and Sellier, Charles E., Jr. (1976) *In Search of Noah's Ark.* Sun Classic Books, Inc., Los Angeles, CA.

Berger, Peter and Zijderveld, Anton. (2009) *In Praise of Doubt: How to Have Convictions without Becoming a Fanatic.* HarperOne, New York, NY.

Bierce, Ambrose. (1958) *The Devil's Dictionary* (Copyright 1911 by Albert and Charles Boni, Inc.). Dover Publications, Inc., New York, NY.

Buckley, Reid. (1999) *Strictly Speaking.* McGraw-Hill, New York, NY.

Calkins, Mary Whiton (compiler). (1913) *The Metaphysical Systems of Hobbes.* The Open Court Publishing Company, Chicago, IL.

Capra, Fritjof. (1991) *The Tao of Physics: An Exploration of the Parallels Between Modern Physics and Eastern Mysticism.* Shambhala, Boston, MA.

Carnegie, Dale. (1936) *How to Win Friends and Influence People.* Simon & Schuster, New York, NY.

Cerf, Christopher and Navasky, Victor. (1998) *The Experts Speak: The Definitive Compendium of Authoritative Misinformation.* Villard, New York, NY.

Darwin, Charles. (1859) *On the Origin of Species by Means of Natural Selection, or the Preservation of Favoured Races in the Struggle for Life.* John Murray, London, England.

Dawkins, Richard. (2006) *The God Delusion.* Houghton Mifflin Company, New York, NY.

Ewen, Pamela Binnings. (1999) *Faith on Trial.* Broadman & Holman Publishers, Nashville, TN.

Fernández-Armesto, Felipe. (1997) *Truth: A History and a Guide for the Perplexed.* St. Martin's Press, New York, NY.

Feynman, Richard P. (1956) "The Relation of Science and Religion," Caltech YMCA Lunch Forum May 2, 1956, California Institute of Technology, Pasadena, California.

Freeman, Charles. (2004) *The Closing of the Western Mind: The Rise of Faith and the Fall of Reason.* Alfred A. Knopf, New York, NY.

Frye v. United States, 293 F. 1013 (D.C. Cir. 1923)

Gardner, William M. (1987) *Language: The Most Human Act.* Center for Social Design, Jacksonville, AL.

George, Henry. (1880) *Progress and Poverty.* Appleton & Co., New York, NY.

Gore, Al. (2007) *The Assault on Reason.* The Penguin Press, New York, NY.

Harris, Sam. (2005) *The End of Faith: Religion, Terror and the Future of Reason.* W. W. Norton & Co., New York, NY.

Hawking, Stephen W. and Mlodinow, Leonard. (2010) *The Grand Design.* Bantam Books, New York, NY.

Hett, W. S. (translator) (1975) *Aristotle: in Twenty-three Volumes, Vol. VIII: On the Soul, Parva Naturalia, On Breath.* Harvard University Press. Cambridge, MA.

Hobbes, Thomas. (See, Calkins, 1913; Jones, 1969)

Hull, Clark L. (1943) *Principles of Behavior.* Appleton-Century-Crofts, New York, NY.

Jaynes, Julian. (1976) *The Origin of Consciousness in the Breakdown of the Bicameral Mind.* Mariner Books, Boston, MA.

Jones, W. T. (1969) *A History of Western Philosophy* (Second Edition), Vols. I, II, III, & IV. Harcourt, Brace & World, Inc., New York, NY.

Kantor, J. R. (1977) *Psychological Linguistics.* The Principia Press, Chicago, IL.

Lec, Stanislaw J. (1962) *Unkempt Thoughts.* St. Martin's Press, New York, NY.

Leggett, Trevor (compiler & translator). (1960) *A First Zen Reader.* Charles E. Tuttle, Co., Rutland, VT.

Martel, Yann. (2002) *The Life of Pi.* Harcourt, New York, NY.

Meehl, Paul E. (1990) "Appraising and Amending Theories: The Strategy of Lakatosian Defense and Two Principles That Warrant It," *Psychological Inquiry,* Vol. 1, pages 108-141.

Muktananda, Swami. (1980) *Meditate.* State University of New York Press, Albany, NY.

Pirsig, Robert M. (1974) *Zen and the Art of Motorcycle Maintenance.* William Morrow & Co., New York, NY.

Roberts, W. Rhys and Bywater, Ingram (translators). (1954) *Aristotle's Rhetoric and Poetics.* The Modern Library, New York, NY.

Rushdie, Salman. (1988) *The Satanic Verses.* Viking Press. London, UK.

Spong, John Shelby. (1991) *Rescuing the Bible from Fundamentalism: A Bishop Rethinks the Meaning of Scripture.* Harper Collins, New York, NY.

Spong, John Shelby. (1999) *Why Christianity Must Change or Die: A Bishop Speaks to Believers In Exile.* HarperSanFrancisco, San Francisco, CA.

Washington, Harriet A. (2011) "Flacking for Big Pharma," *The American Scholar*, Vol. 80, No. 3, pages 22-34.

Wason, P. C. (1966) "Reasoning", in Foss, B. M.: *New horizons in psychology*. Harmondsworth: Penguin, London, England.

Watson, John B. (1924/1925) *Behaviorism*. People's Institute Publishing Company, New York, NY.

Whitaker, Robert. (2010) *Anatomy of an Epidemic*. Crown Publishers, New York, NY.

Zeller, Eduard. (1980) *Outlines of the History of Philosophy*, 13th Edition (translated by L. R. Palmer and revised by Wilhelm Nestle). Dover Publications, Inc., New York, NY.

THE AUTHOR

William Melvin Gardner received both a B.S. in Psychology and a Ph.D. in General Experimental Psychology from the University of Alabama. He taught at Georgia Southern College and Mercer University, and worked in mental health administration in Tennessee and Alabama, before joining the faculty at Jacksonville State University where he taught psychology at the graduate and undergraduate levels. In addition to teaching, he conducted research on topics ranging from comparative psychology to principles of learning to language development. Throughout his professional career and retirement, he remained a student of philosophy, and pursued his hobby of writing automotive history. He lives with his wife, mystery novelist G. P. Gardner, in a small town on Mobile Bay, where they have the time and seclusion to pursue their writing interests.

9 780976 187516